659   2·50

How to plan press advertising

This book is to be returned on or before
the last date stamped below.

LIBREX —

By the same author

Running a Successful Advertising Campaign
How to Plan Direct Mail
How to Plan Exhibitions
How to Plan Radio Advertising
The Perfect Conference
The Business Planner
Business Planning Made Simple
Successful Business Plans in a Week
Correct Letters
Instant Business Letters
Write That Letter!
Tricky Business Forms
Budgeting for Non-financial Managers

How to plan press advertising

Iain Maitland

CASSELL

Cassell
Wellington House, 125 Strand, London WC2R 0BB
127 West 24th Street, New York, NY 10011

© Iain Maitland 1996

First published 1996

British Library Cataloguing-in-Publication Data
A catalogue record for this book is available from the British Library.

ISBN 0-304-33432-4

Designed and typeset by Kenneth Burnley at Irby, Wirral, Cheshire.
Printed and bound in Great Britain by Redwood Books, Trowbridge, Wilts.

Contents

Acknowledgements

I WISH TO ACKNOWLEDGE the help of the following organizations which provided information or assistance in the compilation of this book. Special thanks to those which allowed me to reproduce their material in the text:

The Advertising Standards Authority Limited, and Patrick O'Dee in
    particular
The Association of Media Independents Limited
The Blue Cross, and Sarah Allcock in particular
The Committee of Advertising Practice
The Directory Publishers Association
East Anglia Daily Times Company Limited
Express Newspapers plc, and Michael Moore in particular
Franchise Development Services Limited, and Roy Seaman in
    particular
The Institute of Practitioners in Advertising
International League for the Protection of Horses, and Sarah Bligh
    in particular
IPC Magazines Limited
League Against Cruel Sports Limited, and Anita Cole in particular
Leo Burnett
Media Audits Limited
The National Society for the Prevention of Cruelty to Children,
    and Allison MacDowel in particular
Periodical Publishers Association
Vision Technology Limited, and Jan Murray in particular
Williams and Harmer Partnership, and Mark Aspinall in particular
Young and Rubicam Limited

To Tracey, Michael and Sophie

Preface

HOW TO PLAN PRESS ADVERTISING is written for you, the owner or manager of a prospective, new or existing small firm who is planning to advertise within this medium, possibly for the first time. It begins by introducing the press to you. 'Types of publication' takes a broad overview of newspapers, magazines and miscellaneous publications. 'Who's who in the press' looks inside the press, outside the press and at advertising organizations.

Moving on, it investigates preparing for a press campaign. 'Analysing yourself' shows you how to assess your business, study products and services and look at your short-, medium- and long-term objectives. 'Knowing your market' discusses contemplating customers, evaluating competitors, appraising the marketplace and carrying out any additional research which may be necessary. 'Establishing a budget' tells you how to review the past, consider the present and anticipate the future prior to allocating advertising funds.

The book then guides you through the launch of press activities. 'Bringing in experts' examines commissioning an advertising agency and employing other specialists including a market research company, an illustrator, a photographer and a typesetter. 'Planning your schedule' helps you to list possible publications, compare audiences, think about timing and check out costs before drafting your preliminary advertising schedule. 'Creating advertisements' describes the different types of advertisement, choosing the correct approach, deciding upon layout, selecting copy and staying within the law.

It concludes by turning its attention to running a press campaign. 'Buying advertising space' enables you to read rate cards, negotiate with representatives and deal with publications. 'Conducting your activities' covers administering a trial run, monitoring responses and making changes to your schedule and advertisements. 'The press advertiser's checklist' allows you to reflect upon your knowledge of the press as well as your understanding of getting ready for, commencing and operating advertising activities within this particular medium.

Appendices are incorporated towards the end of the book. A media pack, rate cards, the British Code of Advertising Practice, names, addresses and telephone numbers of useful contacts and a recommended reading list provide you with a comprehensive reference section. With the summaries which complete the chapters, the action checklists and advertisements within the text and a glossary of key terms, this supporting and illustrative material makes the book an essential, hands-on manual throughout each and every press advertising campaign.

Iain Maitland

1 Types of publication

'THE PRESS' IS AN ALL-EMBRACING TITLE which covers a wide and extremely diverse range of newspapers, magazines and miscellaneous publications such as directories, programmes and brochures. Each offers its own distinctive mix of characteristics, advantages and disadvantages to the prospective advertiser. Initially, you need to possess a broad, overall knowledge and understanding of their key features as well as the similarities and differences that exist between them if you are to move on to preparing for, launching and running a winning advertising campaign through the most appropriate publications in your specific circumstances.

Introducing newspapers

Newspapers may be divided up into various categories. There are national dailies such as the *Daily Star*, *The Sun*, and *The Times*, and national Sundays including *The People*, *Sunday Express* and the *News of the World*. There are regional dailies incorporating the *East Anglian Daily Times* and the *Yorkshire Post*, regional Sundays such as Avon's *Sunday Independent* and the West Midlands' *Sunday Mercury*, plus paid-for weeklies and bi-weeklies including the *Burnley Express* and *The Cornishman*, and free weeklies and bi-weeklies incorporating the *Bucks Advertiser* and the *Trent Valley Journal*. Many newspapers, whether regional or national, have several editions. For example, the *Daily Express* and *Sunday Express* print three – for Scotland, the North and the South.

Every regional and national newspaper is as different in its approach to news coverage and reporting as the *Daily Mirror* is to the *Daily Mail,* and *The Sun* is to *The Times*, and are thus more or less attractive to people of either sex, varying ages and social grades – that is, the classes into which the population is grouped according to the occupation of the head of each household (A: upper middle class; B: middle class; C1: lower middle class; C2: skilled working class; D: working class; E: those on subsistence levels). Regionally, newspapers have a relatively widespread and in-depth appeal across and into all sections, developing a close and personal relationship with local people. Nationally, newspapers are more likely to be taken by certain groups, with ABs favouring *The Times*, C1C2s preferring *The Sun,* and so on. Love-hate feelings tend to exist towards many national titles.

The circulation of a newspaper – the number of copies of each issue sold, delivered or handed out – naturally differs enormously according to its individual type. The regionals are circulated to a local area and therefore have much lower figures than the nationals which sell across the country. An average regional newspaper – so far as any publication can be described in such a manner – may have a circulation of perhaps 15,000 to 150,000. *The Cornishman* sells around 20,000 copies each week, the *East Anglian Daily Times* about 50,000 per day and the *Sunday Mercury* approximately 150,000 every weekend. A typical national newspaper – if such a title exists – could achieve a circulation of possibly 500,000 to five million. The *Daily Star* is purchased by around 900,000 people each day and the *News of the World* by over five million every Sunday. As a rule of thumb, Sunday papers – whether regional or national – tend to have larger circulations than dailies because people buy several rather than one title at the weekend for leisure reading.

The 'pass-on' readership of a newspaper – the number of people who look at or read a copy of a publication – is always higher than its circulation, as dailies may be handed to friends and colleagues at lunchtimes or after work, and Sunday papers could be seen by other family members. Weeklies might be left in the office or about the home for a week or so and are usually perused by other people during this period. The readership of any given title might be three to six times more than its circulation, which should be of some considerable interest and relevance to the prospective advertiser.

Advertising costs within regional and national newspapers are closely related to individual circulation and readership figures. Classified advertising – whereby line-by-line advertisements are placed under assorted headings such as 'Goods for Sale' and 'Business Services' – may cost from perhaps £1 to £3 per line in regional papers and from possibly £5 to £20 per line in national papers. The *West Suffolk Mercury* – a free weekly – requires £1.65 for each line and has a circulation of 45,000-plus. The *Sunday Express* charges £16 for its linage with a circulation of two million. Display advertising – where bordered and often illustrated advertisements are located almost anywhere in the newspaper, subject to availability – could vary in price from about £2 to £12 per single column centimetre in the regionals to around £30 to £120 for each single column centimetre in the nationals. A 'SCC' measures one column wide by one centimetre deep. The *West Suffolk Mercury* requests £3.25 upwards per SCC and the *Sunday Express* charges £80 or more per SCC.

There are numerous benefits to newspaper advertising. You can advertise to a broad, cross section of a local population and/or to scattered groups across the country, depending on your requirements. Advertisements may be put under those headings or in the sections or supplements where you believe they will be most effective, subject to availability. The theme, layout and copy of your advertisements can change from one newspaper or edition to another to test the effectiveness of alternative approaches or to pass on a revised message in some areas. Advertisements may be printed on a given weekday or Sunday, allowing you to be topical and/or to convey a sense of 'act now' urgency. You can advertise day after day (or at least week after week) to increase exposure and reinforce your advertising message. Advertisements may be taken at short notice from perhaps two to four days prior to publication so you can quickly place new ones or make amendments to existing ones, according to changing circumstances and unexpected events.

However, various drawbacks exist regarding newspaper advertising. Most people do not read a newspaper from cover to cover nor for any length of time: they flick through and dip into it for about ten to twenty minutes and may therefore miss your advertisement. A significant proportion of readers are probably not interested in your message, so you could effectively be wasting much of your money. The mood of those readers who see and are potentially receptive to your advertisements can vary from harassed and edgy on a crowded train to relaxed and mellow in a warm bath. It is difficult to compose advertisements that are appropriate and equally appealing in all circumstances. Many newspapers have a fairly short lifespan, often left behind on the train after the journey or discarded after the bathwater has drained away, so those advertisements which are not immediately seen and absorbed rarely have a second chance to succeed. The general absence of colour may affect the quality of your message, especially if you wanted to highlight the appearance of your goods.

About magazines

These can be separated into consumer and business titles. Consumer magazines may be broken down further into general consumer titles of widespread, popular appeal and consumer-specific titles for special-interest groups. *Candis*, *The Listener* and *Time Out* may be called general consumer magazines, *Practical Parenting*, *Slimming* and *Waterski International* might be termed consumer-specific magazines. Business titles are usually related to particular products and services, jobs and careers or trades and industries. Hence, *Engineering Lasers* and *Frozen and Chilled Foods* are product associated, *Dairy Farmer and Dairy Beef Producer* and *Teleflorist News* are job related and *Retail Week* and *Sheet Metal Industries* are trade associated. As with newspapers, some magazines have several editions, perhaps for the north, south, east and west of their circulation areas.

Each magazine addresses its own unique mix of topics which attracts various individuals and assorted groups into purchasing and/or reading it. General interest subjects draw in people of both sexes, all ages and social grades, albeit in varying proportions. Special interest topics appeal to those people who share common hobbies, pursuits and/or concerns regardless of sex, age or social grade. Business matters may attract individuals and groups from a sector of a certain trade or from across a number of industries. Each magazine also tackles its blend of subjects in an individual way so that even those titles which appear to appeal to and be bought and/or seen by the same people have slightly different readerships. For example, parentcraft magazines are most popular with expectant women and mothers. *Practical Parenting*'s female readership comprises 76 per cent under-35s, 23 per cent over-35s, 57 per cent ABC1s and 44 per cent C2DEs. *Parents* consists of 74 per cent under-35s, 26 per cent over-35s, 33 per cent ABC1s and 67 per cent C2DEs, which could be of key significance to a prospective advertiser.

A magazine's circulation may be based upon the number of copies sold over the counter, posted to subscribers, handed out to passers-by, pushed through letterboxes or sent free of charge to named individuals (which is more commonly known as controlled circulation). Generally, business titles have relatively low but extremely well-defined circulations, typically ranging from perhaps 2,000 to 50,000. *Sheet Metal Industries*' is approximately 1,700 per issue, *Dairy Farmer and Dairy Beef Producer*'s is close to 26,000. Consumer titles usually have far higher circulations, averaging from possibly 50,000 upwards. *Slimming* sells around 120,000 per issue, compared to 145,000 for *Practical Parenting* and 520,000 for *Candis*. As a rough and ready guideline, the wider a magazine's interests are, the higher its circulation is.

On average, a magazine, whether it is a consumer or a business title, has a readership figure which is ten times more substantial than its basic circulation. As examples, *Parents* has a pass-on readership of 6.6 people, *Vogue*'s is close to the norm at 9.8 whilst *Film Review*'s is well above the average at 18.6. Most magazines are kept until the next one is issued the following week, fortnight, month or quarter. They can be re-read between four to six times by each person during this period.

Advertising rates in magazines are strongly associated with circulation and readership types and numbers. Normally, these titles sell their space by the page – sixteenth, eighth, quarter, half, full-page or double-page spread (two side-by-side pages). Business titles may charge from £200 to £2,000 per page. *Frozen and Chilled Foods*' rate is £725 for a page with a circulation of nearly 4,000 and *Retail Week*'s is £1,980 and has a circulation of approximately 15,000. Consumer titles could demand from £500 upwards for a full page. *Slimming*'s and *Marie Claire*'s rates are £1,230 and £3,100-plus with 120,000 and 155,000 circulations respectively. Hopefully, line and single column centimetre rates may be quoted as well, or need to be swiftly calculated for simpler comparisons between each other's and newspapers' standard rates.

Magazine advertising offers many advantages. You can address clearly defined, small and compact, or large and extensive groups of people who tend to be well informed and interested in your subject. Varied advertisements may be printed in different places within magazines (subject to availability) to maximize potential sightings by the right readers. People often consider 'their' titles to be friends and trusted advisers which gives added credence to any associated advertisements. They also usually look at magazines in a leisurely and therefore receptive mood which makes it easier to compile appropriate advertisements; and they read titles in more detail and for longer than newspapers thus raising their opportunities to see your advertisements. Magazines have a lengthy lifespan, being retained and re-read numerous times; this increases the chances of your advertising message being fully absorbed. Colour is widely available, allowing your advertisements to be more creative, lifelike and appealing.

However, there are several disadvantages to magazine advertising. As many titles are published fortnightly, monthly or thereafter, you cannot advertise day after day or week after week to rapidly build up exposure and awareness of your advertising amongst your potential customers. With advertisements needing to be submitted between one week and a month prior to publication, it is difficult to react swiftly and make changes in response to ever-developing scenarios. Given their lifespans – which goes some considerable way to compensating for these drawbacks – it is hard to predict the exact day or even the week in which your advertisement may be spotted, making it almost impossible if not pointless to create a highly topical advertising message or mood of 'act quickly' urgency which might normally suit your particular needs.

Miscellaneous publications

The press does not simply consist of newspapers and magazines: it is also made up of directories and yearbooks, programmes and brochures, in-house journals, timetables, maps and guidebooks. The sensible press advertiser is aware of, contemplates and, where relevant, makes the most of this hotch-potch of assorted, complementary publications.

Directories and yearbooks – *Carpet Annual*, *Chemist and Druggist Directory* and the *United Kingdom Franchise Directory* amongst them – are reference works covering different trades and industries, which may sometimes double up as advertising media as well. Published regularly on an annual basis in most instances, circulation is relatively low, ranging from perhaps a few hundred to several thousand copies which are distributed to organizations and individuals who are extremely interested in the specific topic. Kept in shops, factories, offices, libraries and about the home for twelve months or more, they may be perused by many people during that time.

In their favour, the majority of directories and yearbooks have status and respectability in their field, giving credibility to those firms which are listed or advertised in them. You can address yourself to a specialized group of readers who are receptive to your message. Knowing your audience and their likely attitudes it is easier to create suitably appropriate advertisements that shall appeal to them. Being retained for a lengthy period, your advertisements may continue to be seen time and again, hopefully reaping enquiries and even sales for as long as five years or more.

However, bear in mind that limited choices exist concerning the size, position, design and contents of advertisements, which might not tally with your personal requirements. Colour is rarely available, which can hinder creativity. Readers dip in and out of these media and are unlikely to spot every business, product or service mentioned within them. Given their longevity, it is unwise to be topical and impossible to promptly amend your advertisement if unsuccessful. Copy deadlines may be six months or so ahead of publication, so advertisements must be planned well in advance as part of an overall campaign.

Programmes and brochures are published for sporting fixtures, leisure events, fund-raising activities and so forth, on a weekly, monthly, quarterly, occasional or one-off basis, as relevant. Their circulation differs enormously depending on circumstances – perhaps from a hundred or so at a village fête through 2,000 at a touring company's week-long run at a theatre to 50,000-plus at a cup final. Buyers are usually closely involved with the associated topic, whether rugby, athletics, a town carnival or cancer research. Programmes and brochures may be seen by several other people who are equally drawn to the related subject, and might be kept as long-term souvenirs of the particular event.

There are benefits in promoting yourself via such media. Varied advertisements – sizes, positions, styles – can be placed, and often in colour for maximum impact. Knowing when and where they will be published and probably read, your advertising message may be up-to-date and highly relevant. Readers are familiar with and knowledgeable in the topic, making the creation and design of advertisements simpler for you. Nevertheless, there are drawbacks too. It is not always easy to remedy unsuccessful advertising as quickly as you might wish, as deadlines may be long and publication only semi-regular or occasional. Although the immediate response to your advertisements may be impressive it tends to drop off rapidly as programmes and brochures are sometimes thrown away soon after being purchased.

In-house journals such as *Barclays News* and *British Airways News* can take the form of newspapers, magazines, newsletters or news-sheets, depending upon the company and its attitude towards internal communications. They may be prepared within the organization or by outside consultants. There are an estimated 20,000 house journals in the United Kingdom, with an overall circulation assessed at approximately twenty million. Typically published once per month, they are seen by employees at all levels within the firm, and sometimes by customers and other business contacts as well.

On a positive note, those journals normally accept advertisements of different sizes, shapes and even colours, positioning them according to the advertiser's wishes. You can sell your appropriately described ideas, products and services to a well-defined, identified audience, and employees tend to assume that advertisers in their title have been vetted and approved, thus viewing them as trustworthy and reputable. Advertisements can also be adjusted at short notice in numerous journals. On the negative side, many titles are of very dubious quality – badly designed, edited and printed – which could reflect upon your concern. Some employees do not read them or do so sparingly, therefore missing your advertisement. Most titles have a fairly short lifespan, being discarded after a brief read.

Timetables are printed for buses, trains, boats, planes and so forth, while maps and guidebooks are published for certain localities and regions. Many of them accept advertisements perhaps from complementary businesses for inclusion alongside or to the rear of the main material. Circulation is typically in the hundreds or low thousands, normally limited to readers who are very interested in the topic related to the publication. Timetables, maps and guidebooks may be passed around and looked at by numerous people and are usually retained for at least a year, if not for much longer.

The key advantages of advertising in these media are that the note of authority which they possess can rub off onto the advertisements inside them. You may promote your concern to a hands-on readership, who are directly involved with the associated subject matter. A lengthy, active life, often of many years, should ensure the advertisements are continually seen over and again. The main disadvantages are that the restrictions upon your advertisements – positions and so forth – may hinder their success; and with long deadlines and lifetimes, it is hard to be topical, make changes or remedy mistakes.

Always contemplate using miscellaneous publications as part of your press advertising campaign: more money is spent on advertising within them each year than on consumer magazines. However, they are a very mixed bag: some are worthy media, others are not. Consider all of them, weighing up the benefits against the drawbacks but don't use them if you feel that the minuses equal or outweigh the pluses. It's not worth risking your money when the traditional and often more reliable media of newspapers and magazines are available.

Summary

1. 'The press' is an all-embracing title which encompasses:
   a) newspapers;
   b) magazines;
   c) miscellaneous publications, such as directories, programmes and brochures.

2. Various types of newspaper exist – national dailies and Sundays, regional dailies and Sundays, paid-for and free (bi-)weeklies amongst them. It is sensible for the prospective advertiser to be aware of their:
   a) approaches to news coverage;
   b) readerships;
   c) circulations;
   d) pass-on readerships;
   e) advertising costs;
   f) benefits for advertisers;
   g) drawbacks for advertisers.

3. Magazines can be separated into consumer and business titles. As with newspapers, would-be advertisers should find out about their:
   a) subject matter;
   b) readerships;
   c) circulations;
   d) pass-on readerships;
   e) advertising rates;
   f) advantages for advertisers;
   g) disadvantages for advertisers.

4. Numerous, miscellaneous publications are often available for advertising purposes – including directories, yearbooks, programmes, brochures, in-house journals, timetables, maps and guidebooks. It is advisable for the potential advertiser to be conscious of their:
   a) individual features;
   b) specific pluses for advertisers;
   c) particular minuses for advertisers;
   d) possible role within a press advertising campaign.

2 Who's who in the press

MOST NEWSPAPERS, magazines and miscellaneous publications are similarly structured, with many departments and employees performing comparable functions and roles within each of them. They are represented by numerous trade bodies and liaise with various advertising organizations which monitor or regulate their activities. You ought to know who's who inside and outside of the press and also be familiar with these other organizations so that you can handle all of them properly, thus maximizing the success of your advertising campaign.

Inside the press

As a would-be advertiser within the Press, it is useful for you to possess a brief understanding of the workings of:

- The Editorial Department;
- The Advertisement Department;
- The Marketing Department;
- The Subscriptions Department;
- The Production Department;
- The Circulation Department.

The Editorial Department

This department is responsible for the contents of the publication – its precise mix of news, features, pictures and advertisements, its attitudes and approaches towards specific topics and so on. It is headed by an Editor-in-Chief who normally has overall responsibility for its success or failure, with assistance from news editors who seek up-to-date news, features editors who co-ordinate occasional and regular articles, and art editors who try to vividly illustrate news stories and feature articles. Beneath them, staff and freelance journalists, illustrators and photographers write copy, produce illustrations and take photographs. Hopefully, they create an attractive and appealing publication to readers and prospective readers, thus boosting circulation and directly raising sales income, and indirectly increasing revenue since a higher circulation usually allows for more substantial advertising rates to be set.

The Advertisement Department

The purpose of this department, and the classified and display advertisement managers and representatives within it, is to sell all of the advertising space for every issue of the publication, at the best possible prices. It works very closely with the editorial department, which probably will have determined the amount, positions, sizes and rates of the spaces available. A difficult and sometimes stormy relationship may exist between editorial and advertisement departments, with editorial staff usually preferring to have less advertising in the publication (whilst recognizing its necessary financial benefits) and advertisement employees requesting additional spaces in improved positions and wanting favourable editorial mentions for advertisers. In theory, if not always in practice, you should receive help from this department when drafting your advertising schedule and designing winning advertisements. See Chapter 7: 'Planning your schedule', page 50 and Chapter 8: 'Creating advertisements', Page 60.

The Marketing Department

Also known as the promotions or advertising department, this performs the key role of publicizing the newspaper, magazine or publication to advertisers and their advertising agencies who may buy space in it, wholesalers and retailers which could stock it and customers who might purchase, subscribe to or take it. The marketing (promotions or advertising) manager and his or her assistants may carry out various, related tasks of particular interest and relevance to you. They could accumulate research data, either from readily available sources, their own findings or specially commissioned surveys about their markets and customers, other media and current and anticipated trends, all of which may be made available to you. Refer to Chapter 4: 'Knowing your market', page 27. They might then promote their publication and services via press advertisements, direct mail shots, exhibitions, guided tours around the premises, and brochures and leaflets, which could enable you to find out if they are suitable titles in which to advertise. Check out Chapter 7: 'Planning your schedule', page 50.

The Subscriptions Department

Many publications – most notably magazines and especially business titles – have a subscriptions department, although some may incorporate it within their marketing or another appropriately named department. Its role in handling readers' subscriptions falls – sometimes uneasily because it occasionally overlaps – midway between the duties of the marketing department which tries to attract buyers and readers and those of the circulation department which distributes copies of the publication. The people who subscribe to a title, probably on a yearly, renewable basis, are not only a fairly regular source of up-front income but also, and often just as important, are a fount of immediately accessible information. The subscriptions manager and his or her staff can ask them about themselves and their likes and dislikes and so forth, and can pass these important details to you. Look at Chapter 4: 'Knowing your market', page 27.

The Production Department

Some newspapers and magazines are conceived, designed and printed on the same premises, with editorial, advertisement and production staff all sharing a work environment. Others – including innumerable miscellaneous publications such as directories – are passed to an independently owned printing works which runs off the required copies of the latest issue before returning them for subsequent distribution. Whether in-house or external production facilities are used, the aim is to produce the publication in the way in which it has been visualized and pieced together by the editorial and advertisement departments, making certain that text, photographs and illustrations are in the correct places and are legible, clear and free of errors.

The Circulation Department

The function of this department, which may be merged into the subscriptions department, is to co-ordinate the tasks of addressing, bundling up and transporting copies of each issue of the publication, whether these total 1,000 or a million. The circulation manager and his or her team have to ensure that the appropriate number of copies are sent out, by post, vans, trains, boats or planes and arrive at the right wholesalers, retailers and/or individuals on time. In all probability you will have little or even no contact at all with the circulation (nor the editorial and production) departments although it is sensible to be broadly familiar with what they do: you may find it beneficial for when you negotiate and deal with the publications that you plan to use in your advertising campaign. See Chapter 9: 'Buying advertising space', page 78.

Outside the press

There are various trade organizations which represent newspapers, magazines and miscellaneous publications. It is helpful to know about the roles, and their relevance to you and your possible press advertising activities, of the following bodies. Refer to Appendix D: 'Useful contacts', page 140, for addresses and telephone numbers.

- The British Business Press;
- The Directory Publishers Association;
- The Newspaper Publishers Association;
- The Newspaper Society;
- The Periodical Publishers Association.

The British Business Press

The BPP – which operates within the Periodical Publishers Association – acts on behalf of the publishers of professional, trade and technical journals within the British Isles. Its over-riding objective is to vigorously promote the main features and benefits of advertising within this specialized medium to advertisers, advertising agencies and the business world. You will therefore find it worthwhile to contact this organization which will answer any queries and will give you assorted data about these particular publications. See Chapter 7: 'Planning your schedule', page 50.

The Directory Publishers Association

The DPA offers full membership to bona fide directory publishers in the United Kingdom, with associate membership available to their consultants and agents, directory printers, compilers and distributors, title owners and overseas directory publishers. The Association's aims include advancing its members' interests, raising the standards and status of directory publishing throughout the country, maintaining a code of professional conduct which members must follow, protecting the public against disreputable and fraudulent practices, and marketing directories as an ideal advertising medium. It is sensible to advertise only in those directories which are issued by publishers belonging to this organization, and who are therefore trustworthy and reliable. On request, the DPA will provide a booklet containing its members' names, addresses and telephone numbers along with details of their various publications. Refer to Appendix E: 'Recommended reading', page 142.

The Newspaper Publishers Association

Representing national newspaper publishers, the NPA seeks to forward their economic and social causes, co-ordinate their activities and supply advice and guidance to them as and where required: training and development, management and staff relations, marketing and advertising and so on. As a consequence, it may be wise to get in touch with this body if you have any questions concerning national dailies or Sundays – answers and supportive material ought to be made available to you. Check out Chapter 7: 'Planning your schedule', page 50.

The Newspaper Society

Acting for regional newspaper publishers, the NS tries to upkeep their reputations, increase co-operation between them on all matters of mutual interest, investigate and report on topics of key significance, and provide information and assistance on major areas of concern such as industrial relations, employment affairs, advertising controls and legislation, training and so forth. For the small business advertiser, the Society is a useful contact because it handles general advertising enquiries, has a database of regional newspaper titles and their circulations, and offers a central production service whereby a single piece of artwork can be converted into different sizes for various newspapers. Look at Chapter 8: 'Creating advertisements', page 60.

The Periodical Publishers Association

The PPA represents consumer and business magazine publishers – in liaison with the British Business Press – regardless of whether their publications are distributed across the counter, by post, subscription or controlled circulation. Its many goals incorporate helping and supporting members and their particular causes, encouraging high standards of media and market research, improving distribution networks, and achieving more advertising and sales for magazine titles. As with the BPP, it is sensible to approach the Association should you want to know more about these publications. Read Chapter 7: 'Planning your schedule', page 50.

Advertising organizations

There are numerous other organizations involved in press advertising with which you ought to be familiar, including the following (please note that their addresses and telephone numbers are listed in Appendix D: 'Useful contacts', page 140):

- The Advertising Association;
- The Advertising Standards Authority Limited;
- The Association of Media Independents Limited;
- The Audit Bureau of Circulation Limited;
- The Committee of Advertising Practice;
- The Incorporated Society of British Advertisers Limited;
- The Institute of Practitioners in Advertising;
- The Joint Industry Committee for National Readership Surveys;
- Media Audits Limited;
- Verified Free Distribution Limited.

The Advertising Association

With its membership made up of many different organizations such as the Incorporated Society of British Advertisers Limited, the Newspaper Publishers Association and the Institute of Practitioners in Advertising, the AA acts on behalf of advertisers, media, agencies and other companies which provide associated advertising services. The Association's main purpose is to champion advertising: to maximize standards at all times, to safeguard its interests, to inform and educate everyone about its role in society and the economy, and to promote universal confidence in it. Of particular relevance to you, the AA can supply information on all aspects of advertising, putting you in contact with specialists when necessary. It also publishes various publications, some of which may be of significance to small-business advertisers.

The Advertising Standards Authority Limited

The ASA is an independent company which oversees the British Code of Advertising Practice – the industry's self-regulatory control system that covers advertisements in printed media and which is based on the precepts that they should be legal, decent, honest, truthful and prepared with a sense of responsibility to consumers, society and competitors. It seeks to ensure that standards are maintained by monitoring the trade, making approximately 150,000 random checks each year and dealing with complaints raised by the public. Those advertisers whose advertisements breach the Code are asked to amend or withdraw them, as appropriate. Failing this, advertisers will find few – if any – publications which are willing to accept the offending, unaltered material. Refer to Chapter 8: 'Creating advertisements', page 60 and Appendix C: 'The British Code of Advertising Practice', see page 131.

The Association of Media Independents Limited

The AMI is the trade body for specialist agencies which deal solely with the planning and purchase of media space and time. They do not offer creative services concerning the style, layout and text of advertisements as traditional advertising agencies do. For small-sized concerns which might employ a media independent, it is sensible to pick one who belongs to this organization. To provide safeguards for advertisers, the Association insists that its members are in the business of media buying, of good professional and sound financial standing as well as being wholly independent of any advertiser, advertising agency or media owner.

These agencies have to demonstrate from client lists and billings that they have capabilities across all media. They must give a written undertaking to supply customers with copy invoices from the media showing the costs of space and time purchased by them. They need to be recognized by the Independent Television Companies Association, the Newspaper Publishers Association and the Periodical Publishers Association and agree to abide by the British Code of Advertising Practice. Copies of their six-monthly and annual accounts have to be filed as proof of their financial status. For more information concerning media independents, look at Chapter 6: 'Bringing in experts', page 42.

The Audit Bureau of Circulation Limited

An independent and non-profit-making company, ABC has a membership of leading publishers, advertisers and advertising agencies. Its purpose so far as the press advertiser is concerned is to certify the circulations of members' publications. It does this by forwarding forms to each publication which must be completed by an independent auditor who is normally the publisher's accountants. On their return to the Bureau, these are checked and if correct an ABC certificate is issued, usually stating the average number of copies sold and/or freely circulated as appropriate each day, week, fortnight or month over the preceding six months. Regular spot checks are made on publishers' records to ensure that auditing procedures are being carried out in the proper manner. It is sensible to be wary of any publications whose circulations are not independently certified, since self-certified statements could be incorrect. Refer to Chapter 7: 'Planning your schedule', page 50.

The Committee of Advertising Practice

The CAP – with its members drawn from all major advertising trade bodies such as the Newspaper Publishers Association, the Newspaper Society and the Periodical Publishers Association – drafts and implements the British Code of Advertising Practice. Its functions include constantly reviewing and amending this Code, investigating complaints made by commercially interested parties (with the Advertising Standards Authority handling the public's grievances) and co-ordinating its members' activities to uphold standards. It gives free, confidential advice to advertisers who wish to know how to correctly interpret the Code's detailed and occasionally complex guidelines. See Chapter 8: 'Creating advertisements', page 60 and Appendix C: 'The British Code of Advertising Practice', page 131.

The Incorporated Society of British Advertisers Limited

Representing national and international advertisers such as British Airways, British Gas and Guinness, the ISBA seeks to advance their causes and promote first-class advertising practices by maintaining an ongoing dialogue with the government, media, advertising agencies and the public. Of special significance to you, it offers advice across a range of subjects including budgets, agency agreements, schedules, costs and so on. Also, it regularly conducts one-day training workshops on topics such as 'Press Media – saving money by effective planning and buying', 'Negotiating with Agencies' and 'Basic Copywriting Skills'. Various, useful books, directories and pamphlets are available as well.

The Institute of Practitioners in Advertising

The IPA is the representative organization of advertising agencies within the United Kingdom, giving its members a broad mix of specialist and information services and highlighting their views in discussions with the government, media and advertising industry. Any small-business person who may consider using an agency ought to choose one which belongs to this body. To join, the Institute stipulates that a would-be member must prove that they can plan and carry out an advertising campaign from start to finish. Consequently, only traditional, full service agencies capable of putting together business and media buying plans, creating advertisements and so forth are eligible, not media independents who simply deal in space and time purchasing.

Accordingly, the IPA checks out the agency's experience – its client base and the type, number and variety of different accounts which are and have previously been handled. Its financial standing and creditworthiness are studied and recognition by other trade organizations is taken into account as well – all of which provide a sense of security for those ventures selecting one of the Institute's members to help them with their advertising. For further details concerning advertising agencies, see Chapter 6: 'Bringing in experts', page 42.

The Joint Industry Committee for National Readership Surveys

JICNARS acts for the Newspaper Publishers Association, the Periodical Publishers Association, the Incorporated Society of British Advertisers Limited and the Institute of Practitioners in Advertising. It controls a national readership survey conducted on a continuing basis among a random sample of approximately 28,000 members of the public. This generates up-to-date information about the Press (plus television, cinema and radio) including the readership of various publications by types of people (analysed by sex, age and social grade), reading frequency and the like. Various reports and bulletins are regularly produced for subscribers which are of particular help to advertisers wishing to promote themselves to the general public. Look at Chapter 7: 'Planning your schedule', page 50.

Media Audits Limited

This independent company offers a consultancy service regarding the best use of advertising media, primarily television and the press. Of key interest to you, advertisers may submit a detailed schedule – type and number of insertions, costs and so on – of their planned advertising within national newspapers and magazines. This is then broken down and analysed with individual positions and prices paid being compared alongside pooled data. An overall assessment of the advertiser's planning and buying performance is then made, for subsequent discussion and future improvements. Check out Chapter 7: 'Planning your schedule', page 50 and Chapter 9: 'Buying advertising space', page 78.

Verified Free Distribution Limited

VFD – and Bulk Verified Services (BVS) which is part of it – is a self-supporting subsidiary of the Audit Bureau of Circulations Limited that certifies the distribution of free publications. Those newspapers, magazines and directories which are delivered to homes are eligible for a Verified Free Distribution certification. Others – distributed in bulk to hotels, stores and miscellaneous pick-up points – may receive a BVS certification. Should you subsequently decide to incorporate the free press within your advertising activities, it is advisable to use only the publications which have VFD or BVS certificates as the uncertified claims of other publications may be unrepresentative and potentially misleading. Refer to Chapter 7: 'Planning your schedule', page 50.

Summary

1. A potential press advertiser should have some knowledge of who's who in the industry, including:
   a) the different departments and employees within a publication;
   b) various trade bodies;
   c) other advertising organizations.

2. Many publications are structured along similar lines and incorporate:
   a) an editorial department;
   b) an advertisement department;
   c) a marketing department;
   d) a subscriptions department;
   e) a production department;
   f) a circulation department.

3. Various trade bodies exist within the industry. In particular:
   a) The British Business Press;
   b) The Directory Publishers Association;
   c) The Newspaper Publishers Association;
   d) The Newspaper Society;
   e) The Periodical Publishers Association.

4. Numerous advertising organizations are involved with press advertising in some capacity. Most notably:
   a) The Advertising Association;
   b) The Advertising Standards Authority Limited;
   c) The Association of Media Independents Limited;
   d) The Audit Bureau of Circulations Limited;
   e) The Committee of Advertising Practice;
   f) The Incorporated Society of British Advertisers Limited;
   g) The Institute of Practitioners in Advertising;
   h) The Joint Industry Committee for National Readership Surveys;
   i) Media Audits Limited ;
   j) Verified Free Distribution Limited.

3 Analysing yourself

YOUR PREPARATION for a press campaign must begin with a vigorous investigation into your business, products, services and objectives. This thorough self-appraisal, when subsequently combined with a detailed knowledge of your market and the careful establishment of a budget, will enable you to make a preliminary assessment of the types of publication which are most likely to be suitable in your individual circumstances. Also, all of this background work ought to allow you to build up sufficient information to move on to commence and administer highly successful advertising activities.

Assessing your business

It is sensible to conduct a wide-ranging, in-depth analysis of your firm, considering its organization, structure and operations. Think about factors such as location with regard to amenities, suppliers, customers and competitors. Contemplate its premises, especially their size, facilities, image and the like. In turn, visit each department – production, finance, personnel, sales – to observe and talk to colleagues and employees about policies, work methods and techniques. Discover everything there is to possibly know, both good and bad, so that you possess a broad and wholly comprehensive understanding of all aspects of your concern.

List the firm's strengths as you see them. Your notes – which will prove absolutely invaluable when you go on to launch your advertising campaign – might typically include comments such as: 'Being my own boss, I can make immediate decisions as I do not have to consult other people; therefore, I am able to run a flexible venture, swiftly introducing new goods, changing suppliers when deliveries are late and varying payment terms to suit customers' needs; the business is well sited close to the industrial estate where most of my clients work, thus I am assured of a high number of quality passers-by; my property is spacious and roomy allowing me to have an extensive product range which draws would-be customers onto the premises; I employ a friendly and knowledgeable team who handle enquiries in an engaging manner, persuasively converting them into sales.'

Detail any weaknesses that you are aware of and calculate how to remedy them, if possible. Your records might incorporate statements similar to these:
'Working alone, I do not have the financial resources to bulk buy for quantity
discounts; as I cannot always compete on price with larger firms I concentrate
instead on offering a prompt, personal service for clients; three months ago, a
national competitor opened a unit which is located only two streets away from
me; in comparison with the same period during last year, my income has fallen
by 35 per cent, largely as a result of this increased competition; I intend to bring
in new lines to compensate for these losses; operating in a seasonal trade, my
fluctuating turnover creates cash flow difficulties for me; I shall have stock
clearance sales at appropriate times to solve these problems.'

Linking together your knowledge of the firm with your appreciation of
the press – see Chapter 1: 'Types of publication', page 1 – should mean that you
are now able to think about where you might advertise, whether nationally or
regionally, in newspapers, magazines or in miscellaneous publications. Read
back over your uniquely individual notes, contemplating the significance of
your business and its particular favourable and unfavourable features so far as
your advertising activities are concerned. Wishing to notify prompt decisions to
customers, perhaps about new stock and changing prices, points to the use of
daily or weekly rather than monthly or quarterly publications. Being based near
to clients' workplaces may suggest the suitability of advertising within in-house
journals so that those people who drive rather than walk to work are reached.
Trading locally could indicate the viability of regional rather than national publications, as might modest financial limits. Completing 'Assessing your business: an action checklist', page 21, may be helpful at this stage.

Studying your products and services

Closely examine whatever you offer or are planning to offer to your customers. Look at your products and services in terms of age, varieties, colours,
sizes, shapes, packaging, uses, prices, quality, safety, reliability, availability,
guarantees and after-sales service, as relevant in your circumstances. Your products and services are of critical importance as most of your advertisements will
probably concentrate on them. Hence, they have to be good: meeting customers'
needs, doing the job properly, being readily available, well-priced and so on.
However excellent your advertisements may be, they will not be able to sell
unwanted or poor quality items (or at least not more than once).

Separate each product's characteristics into pluses and minuses. Consider the benefits – the lowest price, the most reliable performance, two years
parts and labour guarantee – from the customers' viewpoint. You will want to
promote these in your subsequent advertisements to encourage customers to

YOUR FIRM

	Its strengths	Its weaknesses
1. Organization		
2. Structure		
3. Operations		
4. Location		
5. Premises		
6. Departments		
7. Employees		
8. Policies		
9. Work methods		
10. Techniques		
11. Other		

THE PRESS

1. National daily papers
2. National Sunday papers
3. Regional daily papers
4. Regional Sunday papers
5. Paid-for weekly papers
6. Free weekly papers
7. General consumer magazines
8. Consumer-specific magazines
9. Business magazines (product)
10. Business magazines (job)
11. Business magazines (trade)
12. Miscellaneous publications

Assessing your business: an action checklist

buy from you. To coin a phrase, you're selling the sizzle not the sausage. Contemplate any drawbacks that exist as well, seeking to remedy them so far as you possibly can. That sausage needs to taste as good as the sizzle suggests it will do!

Reviewing your detailed product and service notes should help you to revise your initial list of possible types of newspaper, magazine and miscellaneous publication and can be referred to again later on when you start work on your advertisements. See Chapter 8: 'Creating advertisements', page 60. As an example, wanting to illustrate a product's breadth of colours and innovative features would highlight the use of magazines and some miscellaneous publications such as brochures rather than newspapers where colour is less widely available (and if it is, may be of a restricted range and dubious quality as well). 'Studying your products and services: an action checklist' on page 23 may be of interest to you now.

Looking at your objectives

It is wise to set out your precise short-, medium- and long-term business goals in as much depth as you can. These will provide you with the clearest indicators yet of the publications that you may eventually select and, when you move ahead to launch your advertising activities, the ways in which you might successfully run your campaign. They will give you, along with any professional advisers whom you may subsequently commission, a framework to work within and targets to work towards.

Your slightly generalized short-term objectives, some of which could be equally well placed below later headings, might typically include: to promote awareness of our new goods, their key features and uses amongst independent retailers and consumers in the county; to develop a contacts list of potential retail stockists for follow-up mail shots and visits by our sales team; to build up a customer base of 100–125 accounts within the next twelve to eighteen months; to introduce this innovative product range into the region, generating an annual turnover in excess of £200,000 by the close of the second trading year.

In the medium term, goals may be: to recruit appropriate numbers and types of managerial and shop floor staff in readiness for anticipated market expansion; to increase product recognition and understanding amongst all multiple and independent retailers and users across the country; to distribute our goods via as many reputable stockists as possible throughout the United Kingdom; to sell direct to consumers via mail order; to regularly adjust demand when uneconomic sales peaks and troughs occur; to constantly reassure previous and current customers that they bought a winning product or range; to compete against all rivals, gaining and sustaining revenue of £500,000 per annum and a 20 per cent market share by the end of the fifth operating year.

THE PRODUCTS AND SERVICES

Their pluses   **Their minuses**

1. Ages
2. Varieties
3. Colours
4. Sizes
5. Shapes
6. Packaging
7. Uses
8. Prices
9. Quality
10. Safety
11. Reliability
12. Availability
13. Guarantees
14. After-sales service

THE PRESS

1. National daily papers
2. National Sunday papers
3. Regional daily papers
4. Regional Sunday papers
5. Paid-for weekly papers
6. Free weekly papers
7. General consumer magazines
8. Consumer-specific magazines
9. Business magazines (product)
10. Business magazines (job)
11. Business magazines (trade)
12. Miscellaneous publication
13. Miscellaneous publication
14. Miscellaneous publication

Studying your products and services: an action checklist

Your long-term targets, which may be just as relevant if located under earlier headings, could incorporate: to continually remind existing and potential stockists and users of the existence and special qualities of our goods; to notify relevant company and product changes and developments to the market; to uphold the respected name of the firm and the reputation of our goods at all times; to steadily clear out slower-selling products at discount prices; to replace existing goods with equally successful new products before demand for the original range has entered into a permanent decline.

Checking back over your list of objectives will enable you to start thinking about using various publications at different stages, according to what you want to achieve at a particular time. Initially wishing to make local shopkeepers and customers fully aware of your new products points to the maximization of regional press advertising, with some additional activities within business magazines to draw in enquiries from would-be stockists. Then seeking to recruit shopfloor employees indicates the further use of regional newspapers, either weeklies and/or dailies especially if they have a separate section devoted to job advertisements on the same day of each week. National newspapers and/or business magazines may be needed if specialized or managerial positions are to be advertised, which could perhaps be difficult to fill locally. Expanding distribution and sales across the country suggests the possibility of the national press, perhaps backed by the regionals in resisting areas and when new products are again launched, later on.

Filling in 'Looking at your objectives: an action checklist' on page 25 may be beneficial at this point.

Summary

1. Preparations for a prospective press campaign must begin with an investigation of the business, products, services and objectives. This enables:
   a) a preliminary assessment to be made about the types of publication that are most likely to be suitable in the circumstances;
   b) sufficient information to be built up for subsequent use during advertising activities, if appropriate.

2. Assessing the business can be broken down into four steps:
   a) analysing all aspects of it;
   b) listing its strengths;
   c) detailing any weaknesses;
   d) considering the relevance of the press as an advertising medium in this instance.

Short-term objectives   **Types of publication?**

Medium-term objectives   **Types of publication?**

Long-term objectives   **Types of publication?**

Looking at your objectives: an action checklist

3. A study of products and services involves:
   a) identifying all their characteristics;
   b) recognizing their benefits;
   c) understanding their drawbacks;
   d) comparing their key features with those of the different types of publication available.

4. Looking at objectives can be divided into four stages:
   a) setting short-term objectives;
   b) establishing medium-term objectives;
   c) deciding on long-term objectives;
   d) contemplating the suitability of various types of publication at certain times.

4 Knowing your market

M OVING ON with your preparatory work in anticipation of advertising activities within the press, you ought to carry out a study of your existing and/or potential customers, competitors and the marketplace. You need to discover as much as possible about all of them so that you have sufficient knowledge to allow you to further assess the types of publication which may be ideal advertising media in your particular situation. The accumulated market data that you will have gathered together will also consequently help you to approach your imminent press campaign in the most relevant and rewarding manner.

Contemplating your customers

Whether you sell to businesses or to the public, you must seek to obtain a broad understanding of them. You cannot expect to develop a detailed knowledge unless you deal with very limited numbers. With regard to traders, try to find out what you can about their present and future numbers, current and anticipated sizes, locations and activities. For the public, it would be useful to know something about their numbers, locations, sexes, ages, marital status, children, social grades, occupations, incomes and interests, as appropriate. Have a mind's-eye picture of your target customer. For example, 'She is probably a 25–35-year-old housewife, with two children', and so on.

It can also be helpful to check out your customers' habits, so far as you can. Knowing what products and services they buy and when, how often and where they purchase them can be revealing. Understanding which titles they read, when, how often, for how long and what they do with them afterwards could be beneficial too. Their opinions of your organization and products and services (especially the perceived benefits) may be highly relevant to the direction and style of your advertising activities. Attempting to unravel their views of your competitors could be worthwhile as well.

Possessing such background information about your present and/or would-be customers' characteristics, habits and opinions – much of which can be obtained from your own records plus regular correspondence and discus-

sions with them – ought to enable you to think again about the types of publication in which you might subsequently advertise. Look back through your notes
to see if they indicate whether you ought to use the national or regional press,
newspapers, magazines or other miscellaneous publications. Selling to traders
rather than members of the public points to business magazines rather than consumer magazines, and vice versa. Having all of your customers living in a little
village perhaps suggests it would be worthwhile to advertise in the church
and/or women's institute newsletter with the regional press being used if they
are spread across the county and the national press being used should they be
dotted about the country. See 'Contemplating your customers: an action checklist' on page 29 for further help.

Evaluating your competitors

Naturally, it is sensible to wholly familiarize yourself with all of your current and prospective rivals, appraising each and every one of them in as much
depth as you analysed your own firm, so far as this is possible. You certainly
should be able to assess their respective organizations, contemplating their
operations, locations, properties and so on and separating these out into plus
and minus points. Similarly, their products and services ought to be easy to
investigate, viewing them in terms of age, varieties, colours and so forth and
grouping these into benefits and drawbacks. See Chapter 3: 'Analysing yourself', page 19, for more information .

You must also study and carefully evaluate your competitors' past and
present advertising activities within the press, as far as you can, but obviously
you cannot realistically expect to spot each and every advertisement ever
printed. Look at their schedules, including the publications used as well as
when, how often and for how long they advertised. Check out their advertisements too, perusing sizes and positions, the themes and approaches adopted and
the various contents. Refer to Chapter 7: 'Planning your schedule', page 50 and
Chapter 8: 'Creating advertisements', page 60 for fuller details, thus enabling you
to carry out a comprehensive investigation of your rivals' activities.

Knowing all about your competitors – an understanding which should
have developed gradually through many years of reading about and talking to
them and other individuals and firms in the trade – will allow you to further
work upon your list of possible types of publication to use. As an example, you
may be aware that a national rival continually advertises its products in newspapers but never (so far as you can see) in magazines or miscellaneous publications. There must be sound reasons for this and if you correctly assume that
a large competitor is experienced and knows what it is doing, you would be
wise to think about following rather than bucking the trend. 'Evaluating your

OTHER TRADERS	THE PRESS	MEMBERS OF THE PUBLIC	THE PRESS
1. Characteristics:	Type of publication?	1. Characteristics:	Type of publication?
2. Purchasing habits:	Type of publication?	2. Purchasing habits:	Type of publication?
3. Reading habits:	Type of publication?	3. Reading habits:	Type of publication?
4. Opinions:	Type of publication?	4. Opinions:	Type of publication?

Contemplating your customers: an action checklist

competitors : an action checklist' on page 31 may be worth completing at this point.

Appraising the marketplace

It is advisable to build up a broad and detailed appreciation of the main features of the market in which you trade now as well as of those which you may be planning to enter or diversify into at a later stage. Discover the total turnover and overall size of each market in the past, in the present and anticipated in the future. Find out what you can about manufacturers, wholesalers and retailers and their former, current and estimated future market shares. Study the ways in which the market is structured and administered by representative bodies and how its key individuals and companies interact, co-operate and conflict with each other.

You should also look outside the market, becoming aware and remaining ever mindful of the external influences upon it. Political or legal changes such as new government initiatives or statutes may have favourable or adverse effects. So too could social or demographic developments including shifting public opinions, population movements and unemployment. Do not forget the economic situation, especially rising or falling inflation, interest and exchange rates. Technological advances with rapidly improving worldwide communication methods and techniques plus environmental issues such as a shortage of natural resources and pollution could be of relevance as well. You ought to be able to calculate the ways in which these and any other external events will affect your particular marketplace.

By reading back over your lengthy list of internal features and external influences – which will have been relatively easy for you to piece together after years of experience and trading in your chosen field – you ought to crystallize your ideas concerning the assorted publications available to you. In an optimistic market – perhaps encouraged by the prospects of falling interest rates and lower unemployment figures – you may decide to branch out from regional to national newspapers so that you are ready to take a larger share of the expected, increasing sales when they arise. Technological advances which allow newspapers to be printed in a wider range of more realistic colours at a lower price may persuade you to use them instead of magazines in forthcoming campaigns. Refer to 'Appraising the marketplace: an action checklist' on page 33 at this stage.

THE COMPETITORS

THE PRESS

	Their strengths	Their weaknesses	Types of publication?
1. Characteristics			Types of publication?
2. Products/services			Types of publication?
3. Advertising schedules			Types of publication?
4. Advertisements			Types of publication?

Evaluating your competitors: an action checklist

Main characteristics   Types of publication?

Internal features   Types of publication?

External influences   Types of publication?

Likely effects   Types of publication?

Appraising the marketplace: an action checklist

Carrying out additional research

Most of the information that you want to accumulate and write down about your customers, competitors and the marketplace will already be known to you or be easily accessible via sales, financial and miscellaneous records plus formal and informal communication networks. However, there shall inevitably be odd gaps in your knowledge and existing details which will therefore leave you with unanswered questions and incomplete notes. Although these spaces may not adversely affect your hopefully correct choice of publications, they could be detrimental later on when the real significance and true value of all of this work and built-up material becomes fully apparent. If you are to go on to plan a winning advertising schedule, create appropriate advertisements, buy the most suitable advertising spaces and administer successful activities – all developing from these original records – then it is wise to carry out any additional research which is necessary to finalize your notes.

Innumerable local, national and specialist organizations regularly conduct and commission surveys, collect and publish reports and statistics which may contain snippets or even masses of information that could be of relevance and interest to you. Depending on your circumstances, gather up and sift through any material which may be kept by Chambers of Commerce – contact names and details can be obtained from the Association of British Chambers of Commerce. It may be worthwhile visiting libraries too, particularly specialized business ones. The *ASLIB Directory* and *The Guide to Government Departments and Other Libraries* which list these are available from the London Business School Library and the Science Reference Library respectively. Think about getting in touch with local authorities as well – these are much overlooked and underrated sources of substantial reference materials. See Appendix D: 'Useful contacts', page 140, for appropriate addresses and telephone numbers.

Your professional or trade association should be of considerable help to you. *The Directory of British Associations* published by CBD Research Limited and detailing over 6,500 trade organizations in the United Kingdom ought to be referred to in your nearest library if you do not know who or where your representative body is. It is sensible to contact the press itself, its professional associations and other advertising organizations such as the Advertising Association and the Incorporated Society of British Advertisers Limited as they will often reveal their research findings to would-be advertisers. The government with its multitude of departments is probably the biggest producer of useful reports and statistics, which it sells through Her Majesty's Stationery Office. A guide to all government publications can be sent out on request from its Central Statistical Office. Refer to Chapter 2: 'Who's who in the press', page 9, and

Appendix D: 'Useful contacts', page 140, for relevant addresses and telephone numbers.

Consider approaching specialist market research agencies, which exist for the sole or primary purpose of pulling together often exclusive information about customers, competitors and the marketplace on behalf of their clients, many of which are small- to medium-sized businesses. The Association of Market Survey Organisations Limited and the Market Research Society – highly respected and reputable trade bodies representing organizations within this industry – can provide you with useful, general material as well as recommending a number of agencies which are most likely to be able to assist you with your specific requirements. Check out Chapter 6: 'Bringing in experts', page 42, for more details and Appendix D: 'Useful contacts', page 140, for key addresses and telephone numbers.

Summary

1. Would-be press advertisers should continue their preparatory work by studying their existing and/or potential customers, competitors and marketplace. This allows them to:
   a) assess the types of publication which may be ideal advertising media in the particular situation;
   b) accumulate data for consequent use during an advertising campaign, if appropriate.

2. Contemplating customers may be tackled in various ways. It involves:
   a) obtaining a broad understanding of them;
   b) checking out their purchasing and reading habits, plus their opinions on key matters;
   c) thinking about the significance of the press in this instance.

3. An evaluation of current and prospective competitors means:
   a) judging them as fully as possible;
   b) finding out about their past and present press advertising activities;
   c) learning from their activities, successes and failures.

Appraising the marketplace is the next stage. More specifically, it involves:
   a) discovering its internal features and main participants;
   b) identifying the major external influences upon it, and their likely effects;
   c) considering the relevance of the press in such circumstances.

5. Additional information about customers, competitors and the marketplace can be gained from a variety of sources such as:
   a) local Chambers of Commerce and libraries;
   b) trade associations, the press, industry bodies, advertising organizations and the government;
   c) specialist market research agencies.

5 Establishing a budget

C ONCLUDING YOUR LENGTHY and occasionally complex preparation for a possible press campaign, you must review the past, consider the present and anticipate the future before moving on to allocate funds for your planned advertising activities. Having thus completed a comprehensive self-analysis and market study as well as setting your appropriation – as the budget is equally well known – you should then be able to proceed to launch a suitable, winning campaign.

Reviewing the past

If appropriate, consider how much you have spent on advertising in previous years along with the range, number and type of advertisements purchased and their effectiveness, whether in terms of increased enquiries, sales and so forth. Those firms with a limited capacity – perhaps a self-employed painter and decorator or a family-run hotel – and which operate in a constant environment often spend the same sum each year, with allowances made for inflation and higher media costs. From hard-earned experience, they know that it will generate sufficient but not too much business for them. Other concerns trading amidst ever-changing internal and external circumstances should simply use this figure as the starting point from which the correct budget can eventually be calculated.

Some businesses derive their advertising appropriation for the coming year from a percentage of their last annual turnover. The chosen figure which may typically be between 2 and 5 per cent would sensibly be based upon the trade or industry averages uncovered during research. Although it is wise to take this into account when reaching a decision, it is important to bear in mind that last year's turnover might have been especially high or low. High, and it may lead to increased expenditure for this year when it is not necessarily needed; low, and it could result in less money being spent when it is most required, perhaps to reverse or slow a decline in sales.

Contemplate any profits that may remain from last year's trading activities as part or even all of this amount can be used for advertising purposes during the forthcoming annual period. Most firms limit their budget according to what they can actually afford to spend. Realistically, smaller concerns which are restricted by credit terms, overdraft limits and cash flow problems cannot afford to overspend, buying their way out of financial difficulties by extensive advertising. They are unlikely to survive long enough to reap the eventual, undoubted rewards.

Considering the present

Taking your total sales and deducting production and distribution costs leaves you with your gross profit. Consider setting aside a proportion of this sum for your advertising needs. Sensible though it is to link together profits and advertising monies, be mindful that higher sales and the more economic spread of costs leads to a larger gross profit and advertising appropriation with lower sales having corresponding, knock-on effects. Thus, your newly allocated budget may either be excessive or too restrictive for your requirements at this particular time.

Numerous small firms calculate their advertising expenditure by working out the selling price of each individual unit sold, subsequently breaking this amount down between materials, labour, advertising and so on. Planning to sell perhaps 1,000 units in a given period, they then simply multiply the advertising costs within a single unit by 1,000 to finalize the appropriation. Analysing this method, you need to recognize that it may be worthwhile in the short term, but less so later on. Internal and external costs rarely remain constant and in line with each other for long, so they have to be monitored on an ongoing basis, and revised time and again.

Difficult though it is to assess your rivals' advertising budgets, you ought to attempt to estimate what they are. Of course, you cannot know for sure because it is unlikely that you can check each publication on the market and ascertain and add up the cost of every advertisement. Nevertheless, from the promotional activities which you have seen, you may be able to hazard very approximate minimum and maximum figures. Clearly, such information can be more useful than having none at all. You may then decide to set an appropriate, high appropriation if you are seeking to seize a larger share of the market.

Anticipating the future

Forecasting your sales for the upcoming quarter, six months or year, you may choose to put by a percentage of this to pay for your advertising campaign. Selecting a figure which is close to the across-the-board, trade average is wise. See Chapter 4: 'Knowing your market', page 27. Nevertheless, the success or failure of this budgeting method is largely dependent upon the accuracy of your forecast. Also, more advertising is likely to take place in boom times when sales are at a peak rather than during lean periods when it might be most needed.

Many concerns estimate the profits that may be generated in their next accounting period and then allot some of this amount for their advertising during this time. Relating the appropriation to future profits is a sound approach in principle, but often not in practice. If profits are overestimated and too much money is spent on advertising, cash flow problems can result, especially for smaller ventures which are running on limited finances. It is therefore advisable to continually review sales, costs and profits, adjusting advertising expenditure as and where necessary.

Setting your short-, medium- and long-term business goals – whether to attract 5,000 enquiries, sell 1,000 units or clear out all of your remaining stock at cost prices – you will naturally wish to set a budget which is substantial enough to achieve these objectives. See Chapter 3: 'Analysing yourself', page 19. Naturally, it is hard to calculate the minimum sum which needs to be spent to fulfil your targets. It is tempting to spend excessively to try to ensure success with money wasted on larger and more frequent advertisements in different positions and for longer periods for few additional enquiries or sales. Refer to Chapter 7: 'Planning your schedule', page 50.

Allocating advertising funds

Whatever your favoured approach, always budget well in advance – typically for the next twelve months – and establish a flexible, financial framework in which you can consequently plan an advertising schedule and advertisements for the same period. Check out Chapter 7: 'Planning your schedule', page 50 and Chapter 8: 'Creating advertisements', page 60. For some advertisers, the approximate amount which ought to be allocated will be readily apparent, based on a calculating method – a percentage of earlier sales, a proportion of previous profits and so on – that seems to be most relevant in the circumstances. The craftsman who works alone manufacturing handmade goods knows he can only produce so many models and that advertising in a certain publication at given times will generate enough orders for his business.

More likely though, you will be unable to decide how much or how little money should be made available for your advertising needs. It is sensible to work out the respective sums which would be budgeted if you followed each of the main methods, subsequently comparing and contrasting the resultant figures. Taking the lowest and highest amounts, you could then set minimum and maximum financial limits for your advertising activities, perhaps pencilling in various proportions between departments, products and services, types of publication, times of the year and so forth. Initially plan to spend a sum which is close to your lower limit, thus keeping funds in reserve for appropriate special offers which may unexpectedly arise for advertising at short notice in one-off or seasonal supplements or for taking space left free as a result of last-minute cancellations by other advertisers – see Chapter 9: 'Buying advertising space', page 78.

Ask or instruct your colleagues and employees, if relevant, to keep you fully informed on a continuing basis of possible developments and changes which may occur both inside and outside your firm, with particular regard to your production capabilities, overheads and costs, selling prices, sales levels, profits, sales targets and expectations, the trading environment, competitors' (estimated) budgets and customers' responses to your advertising. All of these factors could influence your appropriation to varying degrees. Be prepared to review each and every one of them in successive quarters and if necessary update your minimum and maximum figures for the next year. Completing 'Allocating advertising funds: an action checklist' on page 41 is a good idea at this stage. You will find it useful.

Summary

1. Preparations for a possible press campaign may conclude with the establishment of a budget. This task can be completed by:
   a) reviewing the past;
   b) considering the present;
   c) anticipating the future;
   d) allocating appropriate funds for advertising activities.

2. A budget can be set in relation to the past, being based upon:
   a) earlier advertising appropriations;
   b) a percentage of previous sales;
   c) a proportion of earlier profits.

3. Some would-be advertisers calculate a sum on the basis of what is happening at the present time, relating it to:
   a) current profit levels;
   b) existing selling prices;
   c) competitors' estimated budgets.

4. A budget can be established with regard to the future, being linked to:
   a) a percentage of upcoming sales;
   b) a proportion of expected profits;
   c) short-, medium- and long-term goals.

5. Advertising funds should:
   a) be set well in advance;
   b) take account of the different budgetary approaches;
   c) have minimum and maximum limits;
   d) be flexible enough to allow for changing circumstances.

Method	Relevance/Irrelevance	Possible figures	Minimum-maximum sum
1. Previous budgets?			
2. % past sales?			
3. % past profits?			
4. % cost price?			
5. % selling price?			
6. Rivals' budgets?			
7. % future sales?			
8. % future profits?			
9. By objectives?			

Allocating advertising funds: an action checklist

6 Bringing in experts

C OMMENCING THE LAUNCH of your forthcoming press activities, you ought to consider commissioning an advertising agency and think about employing other specialists, such as a market research agency, an illustrator, a photographer, a copywriter and a typesetter who may be able to help you to maximize the success of your press campaign. Although most small-business advertisers conduct their own activities by mixing together in-house knowledge and experience with some assistance from the various departments within each publication, it is useful to be aware of these independent experts and their roles, the services that they can provide and the ways in which they should be assessed and subsequently chosen by you, if relevant.

Commissioning an advertising agency

There are several, rather generalized types of advertising agency which can assist you with your activities. A 'full service' agency offers a broad and diverse range of different services, typically including market research, marketing, media scheduling, advertisement design and creation plus media buying. An 'à la carte', or 'creative', agency usually concentrates on pulling together winning advertisements instead of becoming involved in media planning, negotiating and purchasing. Some à la carte agencies work in tandem with a 'media independent' – another type of agency – which does not provide creative services but devotes itself to buying the best space (and time) available from a variety of media at the most advantageous prices. Numerous agencies – whether full service, à la carte or media independent – specialize in certain trades (financial, recruitment and so on), products and services (such as newly developed items and industrial goods) and individual media (television, posters and the like).

If you are considering the possibility of hiring an agency to help with or even take control of your advertising activities, you initially need to decide which type (if any) is likely to be most suitable for you in your specific circumstances. Already having comprehensively assessed the key strengths and weaknesses of your own venture and being aware of the support which may be offered to you by assorted departments within newspapers, magazines and miscellaneous publications, you should be able to swiftly conclude whether you ought to have either the whole campaign run by an independent agency, part of it such as creative or space buying services or none of it at all.

Conscious of the type of agency which you wish to employ and the work that you expect to be carried out on your behalf, think about the main characteristics which you want to see in your chosen agency. You may believe that it must be reputable, with an ethical approach to business and financial stability so that it shall not handle competing accounts, will disclose conflicting interests to you, shall offer impartial advice, will maintain your confidentiality, and shall not suddenly collapse taking any of your deposited funds with it. Belonging to and/or being recognized by respected trade bodies and supplying sound references should be sufficient proof of this. Previous knowledge and experience of your type of concern, goods and services, customers, competitors and/or markets could be a requirement too, in order that its team knows how to piece together an appropriate schedule for you, is familiar with what succeeds and fails in your field and has tackled and hopefully overcome common problems before. Finding out about its years in business, key executives and personnel, former and existing clients and past and present campaigns should provide enough evidence for you.

Creativity may be an important quality to look for in an advertising agency so that advertisements which are designed by its staff convey your message in a fresh and original way, rather than simply rehashing old and oft-used ideas. Learning about the agency's creative team – their backgrounds, qualifications, earlier work, thoughts and opinions – ought to reveal the answers to you. Compatibility is another, often overlooked attribute which is worth seeking, with you, your employees, agency personnel, in-house and agency tasks all needing to dovetail and pull in the same direction if your campaign is to be a winner. Sharing common ground – perhaps similar-sized firms trading in the same region – and being able to quickly establish a warm, working relationship, swiftly understanding what each party wants and expects from the other are all favourable signs for the future.

You have to be sure that the agency offers you value for money and does not exploit your inexperience in certain areas by overcharging you for its services. It is wise to familiarize yourself with the ways in which agencies are paid, just before going on to shortlist them and meet their employees. Not surprisingly, no hard and fast rules exist. Some agencies receive commission at around 15 per cent from the publications in which advertisements are placed, and are satisfied with that sum. Effectively, you are receiving the agency's expertise free of charge, as that commission would not be deducted from your total bill even if you had dealt direct with the titles. Others require an additional amount for

their services if this revenue does not cover their workload, perhaps when com-
missions are below 15 per cent as they are from various titles. Numerous agencies ask for a flat annual fee and/or submit invoices for their work, based on
hourly or daily rates. Make certain that you are aware of an agency's policy and
are happy that it is fair to you before asking them to act.

Draw up a shortlist of potentially suitable agencies by contacting the
Institute of Practitioners in Advertising and the Association of Media Independents Limited. These leading trade organizations will supply you with lists of
their trustworthy and reputable members as well as providing other, miscellaneous information and advice about making the right choice of agency for you.
Reading through the brief notes about each individual agency, pick out those
which appear to have the qualities that suggest they may fulfil your criteria –
perhaps small but growing concerns which are near to you and so on. Write to
or telephone each one in turn, arranging to meet an accounts executive – the person who is responsible for dealing with clients and acting as an intermediary
between them and the agency – to discuss a possible commission. Hopefully,
you will have at least one meeting with accounts executives, or directors in
smaller businesses, of perhaps three to six agencies from which you will eventually make your final choice.

At a first meeting with an accounts executive – which should ideally be
on your premises – you ought to tell him or her all about yourself so that ideas
can be accurately formulated and valid suggestions subsequently made about a
proposed advertising schedule and/or prospective advertisements for you. Discuss your business and hand over accompanying notes and documentary data
such as sales and financial records concerning your business, its products and
services, your objectives and advertising appropriation. Be as open and detailed
as possible so that the agency has the raw materials needed from which to develop quality plans and proposals on your behalf. Talk – and back up your comments with supplementary notes and supporting evidence such as research
findings – about your customers, competitors and the marketplace.

To convey a fuller and more precise impression of yourself, show the
accounts executive around your property and/or various outlets so that he or
she can see how it is organized and run, look at its location and facilities, sit in
on discussions and meetings (perhaps about goals and budgets), watch different
departments operating and liaising with each other and chat to your colleagues
and employees, especially to those who will be involved with advertising in
some capacity. Encourage the accounts executive to examine and use your products and to see services being performed. Allow the executive to meet and talk
to your customers, perhaps by standing behind a counter with an experienced
member of staff or by spending time on the road with sales representatives or
agents. Explain where your competitors are based (if relevant), so that the

executive has the opportunity to visit and assess them, which may be of some assistance when the agency puts together advertising proposals for your approval.

Naturally, you also wish to discover more about the advertising agency in order that you can decide whether it possesses the key characteristics which you are seeking and if its staff are able to carry out the work that you want them to do for you. During your meeting, ask questions such as: How long have you been trading for? When did you join your representative body? Do you act on behalf of any of my competitors? Will you have conflicting interests by working for me? Are you recognized by other trade organizations? How is your agency structured? Who are your directors? What are their backgrounds, qualifications and areas of expertise? How many people work for the agency? What are their career histories? What exactly do each of them do? Who do you represent, and who have you represented, particularly in my field? What campaigns are you, and have you been, working upon? Do you have any examples of your recent and present work with you? May I have the names and addresses of the companies which you are currently acting for? What are your terms and conditions of work? The answers to these queries – subtly drawn into your amiable conversation – will enable you to start taking the agencies in order of preference.

Work through all of the responsibilities and tasks which you hope to hand over to your selected agency – space planning and/or buying, advertisement creation and design and so on – making certain that both parties are wholly familiar with what the other side seeks and needs from them, to avoid overlapping activities, confusion and possible ill-feeling later on. Providing written confirmation of verbal requests and expectations, offering assistance without interference, supplying up-to-date information on any relevant developments, changes and problems, and delivering work and paying bills on time are likely to be mutually agreed requirements for working together well. Ask the executives of your favoured agencies if they would like to prepare outline proposals for presentation and analysis at a second meeting and whether you may obtain references from your choice of its past and present clients. The remaining executives – who will probably concur with you in your decision that the two parties are ill-matched – need to be thanked and rejected graciously.

Follow up meetings with the account executives or directors of your first and second choice agencies ought to be conducted at their offices so that you can further assess them in their own working environment. Ask to be shown around the property, paying a visit to the market research, marketing, media planning, media buying and creative departments in turn (although these may be amalgamated or even merged into one within smaller agencies). Look at the overall appearance of the premises and equipment, ranging from old and tatty to new and in mint condition. Listen to the comings and goings; hopefully the agency is constantly busy, with telephones ringing and an air of controlled chaos. Learn from the atmosphere, whether cold and frosty or friendly and co-operative. Seeing the agency at work will help you to decide how reputable, financially stable, compatible and so on it really is.

Talk to the agency's staff, especially the media planner and buyer, copywriters and artists who are mainly responsible for preparing your provisional advertising schedule and proposed advertisements. Still wishing to know more about them, you ought to raise queries such as: What do you do? What work and advertising experience do you have? What are you working upon at the present time? How is that progressing? Why did you choose to draft this schedule? How did you think of these advertising ideas? What have you previously worked on in my particular field? How successful were those campaigns? What are the do's and don't's of advertising in my given territory? What suggestions do you have for my advertising activities? The replies to these questions – which will need to be carefully timed and phrased – should give you the necessary insights into the team's characters and qualities.

Your visit should then conclude with a brief presentation by the agency's team, setting out their thoughts about and proposals for your potential schedule and advertisements. Typically, they would discuss and explain their views on the newspapers, magazines and miscellaneous publications which they believe should be used; the sizes, positions, approaches, layouts and contents of your advertisements; the timing, frequency and duration of your activities; as well as the total costs which would be incurred. Contemplate and respond to their comments, trying to appraise whether their plans are realistic, original and viable, showing an appreciation and understanding of your business situation, wants and needs and financial circumstances. Take away a written copy of their ideas for later, quiet consideration and assessment. See Chapter 7: 'Planning your schedule', page 50 and Chapter 8: 'Creating advertisements', page 60 for further information.

Having attended various meetings and studied your first and reserve choice agencies' proposals at length, you now should be able to settle on which one is most reputable, experienced, creative, compatible, cost-effective and so on. Confirm your decision by taking up references for your probable choice, telephoning rather than writing to the referee to increase the likelihood of more realistic, off-the-record opinions being made. These questions should be posed: Has the agency always acted in a reputable and ethical manner? – if 'No', what happened? How relevant have its suggested schedules been to your particular situation? How successful have its advertisements been for you? How well do you get along with its staff on a personal level? Have you had value for money from the agency? Have you experienced any problems with the agency or its team? – if 'Yes', what happened? Will you use the agency again? In the light of these answers, you ought to be in a position to commission the best agency for you, whilst politely declining the services of the others.

Employing other specialists

If you prefer not to work with an advertising agency, you may instead refer to numerous other experts either now or at an appropriate later date to assist in some capacity with your press campaign. A market research company could seek out additional data concerning your customers, competitors and marketplace which you were unable to uncover. An illustrator might design attractive artwork, a photographer could produce eye-catching photographs, a copywriter may draft interesting text, and a typesetter could provide distinctive typefaces to choose from if they have not already been specified by the illustrator (as sometimes happens). All of these people can help to make your advertisements more effective. Look at Chapter 8: 'Creating advertisements', page 60.

Consider which of these specialists (if any) may be of value and of active assistance to you. Gaps in your knowledge of the market could prove to be damaging, if not fatal, to the quality of your forthcoming schedule and advertisements. For example, being unaware of your customers' readership habits and their perceptions of your goods might lead to inadequately detailed advertisements in unread publications. You may not have the in-house facilities to create appealing advertisements and could suspect that staff working for the innumerable titles in which you might advertise do not possess the flair or inclination to produce fresh and distinctive ones on your behalf. Even if you can handle all of your advertising activities yourself, it is still wise to liaise with experts so that you can derive a broader and more complete understanding of the ways in which advertising works.

Obtain the names, addresses and brief details of regional market research agencies from their leading trade organizations – the Association of Market Survey Organisations Limited and the Market Research Society. Build up a localized list of other specialists by contacting the Association of Illustrators, the British Institute of Professional Photography, the British Printing Industries Federation and the Society of Typographic Designers. See Appendix D: 'Useful contacts', page 140 for the addresses and telephone numbers. More data and personal recommendations should be forthcoming from well-informed business colleagues and associates which ought to enable you to shortlist half a dozen experts who are worth talking to.

Your discussions with candidates – on the telephone and at face-to-face meetings at each other's offices – should unfold along similar lines to your earlier negotiations with advertising agencies. You will sketch out the key qualities that you wish to recognize in them, more often than not expecting respectability, a working knowledge of your field, a lively imagination, an understanding of your individual traits and problems plus fair and reasonable charges. Then, you will want to get to know each of them as well as you possibly can, seeing how far they match your set criteria by asking gently probing questions, looking around their premises, talking to their employees, studying their work and so on.

At the same time, these experts – whether market researchers, illustrators, photographers, copywriters or typesetters – may (or certainly ought to) wish to know more about you in addition to the various tasks that you want them to carry out on your behalf. Accordingly, you will need to chat, and could be questioned, about your firm, goods, short-, medium- and long-term targets and budget, as well as your customers, main rivals and markets, as relevant to the particular specialists. Obviously, a copywriter may need to possess an in-depth, working knowledge of all of these aspects if he or she is to produce the right approach and copy for your advertisements, whereas a typesetter could simply seek to find out how you wish your venture to be perceived in the marketplace so that appropriate typefaces can be recommended. Walk them around your property or units, supplying products for examination, introducing customers and handing over market details where necessary.

Clarify and discuss the work that you intend to allocate to them, possibly to ascertain what your present customers really think of your services, to photograph you and your management team or to set out advertisements in a variety of ways so that you can finalize a house style. Explain precisely what you are looking for from them, by when and for how much money. Check out what they want from you – no amateur interference, regularly updated data and so forth. Go through their ideas and suggestions to see which are likely to be most fitting in your situation. Ask for the names, addresses and telephone numbers of their former and current clients, requesting permission to approach two or three for references. Contact these referees to substantiate your thoughts, consequently commissioning the most suitable expert to work alongside you, and rejecting the others in a polite and amicable manner.

Summary

1. Although most press advertisers conduct their own activities with some assistance from the publications they use, a proportion do take additional expert advice. It is sensible to have some knowledge of:
    a) commissioning an advertising agency;
    b) employing other specialists.

2. When commissioning an advertising agency, prospective advertisers should:
   a) identify the type of agency they wish to work with: typically, full service, à la carte or media independent;
   b) decide on the work that the agency is expected to carry out;
   c) think about the characteristics that the agency should possess;
   d) draw up a shortlist of reputable agencies by contacting trade bodies;
   e) meet accounts executives on home territory to find out about each other, and the campaign – some agencies can be rejected politely at this stage;
   f) visit first- and second-choice agencies for further discussions and the presentation of ideas;
   g) take up references before making the final choice.

3. Employing other specialists should be approached in a careful and conscientious manner. Would-be advertisers need to:
   a) consider the type of specialist required – perhaps a market research company, illustrator, photographer, copywriter or typesetter;
   b) contemplate the work that they are required to do;
   c) specify the key qualities that the particular specialist should have;
   d) shortlist by contacting the appropriate, representative bodies;
   e) meet the shortlisted specialists to discuss each other, and the proposed activities;
   f) obtain references prior to reaching a selection decision.

7 Planning your schedule

CONTINUING WITH THE LAUNCH of your imminent press campaign, you and any professional advisers with whom you may be working need to list the publications which you might use, subsequently comparing your audience, thinking about timing, and checking out costs prior to drafting them into a schedule. It is now that all of your extensive and detailed preparatory work – thoroughly analysing yourself, getting to know the market and carefully establishing a budget – will prove wholly invaluable to you. Always refer back to any previous notes which you may have made, whilst slowly piecing together your preliminary schedule.

Listing publications

Begin by setting down the different types of publication, from national daily newspapers through business magazines to house journals, which may conceivably be appropriate advertising media in your particular situation. Reflect again upon your own venture, its goods and services and your goals to convince yourself that these various publications really seem to be relevant to you. Similarly, think about your customers, competitors and the marketplace for the same reason. Contemplate your advertising appropriation as well, since some publications may simply be too expensive for your financial circumstances.

Beneath the varied headings of national dailies, national Sundays, regional daily newspapers and the like, you then have to discover and write out all of the many titles which exist within each category. To draw up a full and comprehensive list, refer to *British Rate and Data* – or BRAD as it is more commonly known – which is a 600-page directory that provides extensive details of the widest possible range of newspapers, consumer and business publications, as well as broadcast, electronic and outdoor media, within the United Kingdom. Published each month by Maclean Hunter Limited, a typical entry would include information about publication and copy dates, advertising rates, mechanical data, circulation and key executives. See Appendix D: 'Useful contacts', page 140 for the address and telephone number.

Additional data about these titles and other, miscellaneous publications – directories, yearbooks, house journals and the like – may be derived from your friends, colleagues and/or full service, à la carte advertising agency or media independent. Also contact the numerous press representative bodies such as the Directory Publishers Association, Newspaper Publishers Association and Periodical Publishers Association, plus those other press organizations including the Audit Bureau of Circulation Limited, Joint Industry Committee for National Readership Surveys, and Verified Free Distribution Limited – all will supply useful background material to you.

Moving ahead, you should contact the advertisement director or manager of each title requesting a media pack, rate card and a copy of the most recent issue if you have not seen it. A media pack, or marketing or media guide as it may be called, is a brochure or booklet which is published by many leading newspapers and magazines, setting out detailed information about the publication (its price, regular columns, features, supplements and so on), its circulation (including the total number, sexes, ages, social grades, occupations, activities and interests of the population) and its readership (incorporating the total number, sexes, ages, plus readership habits and opinions of the title). Look at Appendix A: 'Media pack', page 93, for further details.

A rate card – sometimes incorporated within a media pack – is a double-sided sheet or pamphlet which is available from all reputable publications. It lists data such as display, classified and special position advertising rates, circulation and readership figures, perhaps including demographic and/or regional breakdowns, copy deadlines, on-sale dates, the names, telephone extension numbers of key personnel, technical and mechanical information and the conditions of acceptance of advertisements. See Appendix B: 'Rate cards', page 111, for examples from various newspapers, magazines and miscellaneous publications.

Possessing a copy of the latest edition of the title will enable you to study and carefully assess its editorial and advertising matter. It may even be sensible to obtain several issues, possibly over a number of months, to fully appreciate its individual style and approach and to see how it changes during this period of time. Such a hands-on knowledge of each publication when linked with the information available in the media packs and the rate cards will allow you to go on to fully analyse the titles in which you want to advertise. It will also be particularly helpful to you when you begin to sketch out prospective advertisements. Refer to Chapter 8: 'Creating advertisements', page 60.

Comparing your audience

In turn, you must check through the assorted media guides and rate cards, noting the circulation and readership figures and breakdowns of every publication on your list. Hopefully, this in-depth information will have been independently confirmed by the Audit Bureau of Circulation Limited, Verified Free Distribution Limited or Bulk Verified Services so that it can be wholly trusted and relied upon. Next to each individual set of facts, write out the business and/or personal characteristics of your customers. These details ought to be available from your previous analysis. Having side-by-side data in front of you about your customers and the respective audiences will enable you to compare and contrast them in a competent and thorough manner.

Study the profile of each newspaper's, magazine's and miscellaneous publication's audience alongside your own, working through all of the twin sub-headings to assess how closely the overall make-up of one matches or clashes with the other. Clearly, you are looking to retain titles on your list which are purchased and read by those people who match your customer profile whilst deleting the rest. Also evaluate how far each publication penetrates into your audience, calculating the number and percentage of your customers that it will reach. Naturally, you are seeking to advertise only in those titles which are perused by the highest possible proportion of your target market, and will exclude the remaining ones from your plans.

It is important that you appraise individual publications strictly on the grounds of profile and penetration rather than on high or low circulation and readership figures alone, as so many first-time and naive advertisers do. No matter how many copies of a title are sold or how many times they are seen, they have to be read by the right type and number of customers if your advertising activities are to be successful. It is a waste of your time, money and efforts to direct a message towards people whose response is to largely ignore it. Having completed profile and penetration assessments and reduced your original lengthy list of publications, you should then be able to move ahead to look at the timing of your press advertising campaign. Fill in 'Comparing your audience: an action checklist' on page 53 at this stage. It is helpful.

Thinking about timing

You must carefully consider when you should advertise, perhaps before and/or during a particular week, month or quarter. Obviously, your timing depends mainly upon your business, products and services and objectives. Referring back to your earlier notes will help you to make the right choice for you. Regularly introducing new lines, holding stock clearance sales, preparing to launch an updated product, selling seasonal goods and wishing to adjust sales peaks and troughs indicate certain times to you. Timing will also be strongly influenced by your customers, competitors and the marketplace. Looking through those previous records will provide you with some answers. Dealing

The publication's audience

1. Characteristics

2. Purchasing habits

3. Reading habits

4. Opinions

5. Other

The target customers

1. Characteristics

2. Purchasing habits

3. Reading habits

4. Opinions

5. Other

Comparing your audience: an action checklist

with customers who spend most of their money at the end of a month, knowing that large and experienced national rivals advertise at, presumably, the best given times, and being aware of imminent legislation which might affect demand, all point towards specific periods which are fitting in your circumstances.

It is sensible to think about how often you ought to advertise, possibly daily, weekly or fortnightly. The frequency of your advertising should be affected by your specific situation – firm, goods, goals and so on – as summarized in those accumulated notes. New ideas and developments whether in your concern, products or services usually indicate that rapid promotion is needed if they are to be absorbed and accepted by customers who are generally slow to become accustomed to innovations of any kind. Oft-purchased goods normally require more repetitive advertising than slower-selling products so that customers are continually reminded of them and their benefits just before or when the buying decision is being made. Seasonal and fashionable goods which are available or popular for only a short time before entering a sudden and sharp decline have to be vigorously promoted if they are to make and briefly sustain a sales impact. Ever-changing customers and market conditions suggest the need for increased advertising if recognition and understanding of your business and its products are to be maintained.

You have to contemplate for how long you should advertise. The duration of the advertising activities again ought to be decided by your individual circumstances as outlined in your thorough records. You may feel that short, quick-fire bursts of advertising are appropriate for you, perhaps to coincide with your brief clearance sales, the availability of a seasonal or fashionable range of goods and services, or the necessity to boost sales for a limited period of time. Alternatively, you could think that long-term, steady advertising is more relevant, possibly if you are always adding to your stock on an ongoing basis, and are seeking and are happy with constant turnover throughout the year.

It is then necessary to check the copy deadlines of the various titles, as set out in the rate cards in front of you. Bearing in mind how far in advance you must submit material to some publications, especially glossy magazines and directories, you may discover that you have insufficient time in which to prepare your advertisements and could have to delete numerous titles from your steadily shortening list. Get in touch with the advertisement departments of the publications left to make certain that you will be able to advertise when, as often and for as long as you want to. Many newspapers, magazines and miscellaneous publications have some of their advertising space booked on a semi-permanent basis, with others promptly taken, especially at the most popular times. You may find it difficult to pick and choose titles you advertise in as you would have hoped to have been able to do.

Checking out costs

You must consider the sizes of your advertisements, making sure that you book advertising spaces which are big enough to carry your message and to be seen by your customers, whilst still incurring acceptable costs. Reviewing your various notes should provide some clear pointers for you. Running a certain type of business may indicate that a particular size is most appropriate in the situation – you could believe that a large advertisement is required to convey the correct image of your prestigious business. Perhaps you wish your goods to be illustrated to highlight their key features or want to explain their many uses, all of which needs substantial room if the advertisements are to be effective. Your customers' readership habits – uncovered by you or a market research company acting on your behalf – should reveal which sizes are seen and not seen, as relevant. Your competitors' advertisements – small or large – could influence you as well, especially as you are trying to keep pace with or ahead of them in the marketplace.

It is wise to think about the positions of your advertisements, seeking to maximize their chances of being spotted and read by customers, whilst minimizing their prices so far as possible. Those detailed records ought to be of further assistance to you. Owning a garden centre may suggest that advertisements on or near to a regular horticultural page would be successful, a nightclub could be promoted in a 'What's On' supplement and so on. Similarly, your goods may be best advertised in or close to various sections – a fashion column, business news, television and radio pages for example. Your goals should provide some ideas too, with new staff being sought via advertisements in special recruitment features. Your findings concerning the readership habits of your customers may be decisive factors in your choice of positions. Typically, they would indicate that advertisements towards the front, rather than the back of a publication, alone instead of alongside other advertisements and at the top in preference to the bottom, to the right instead of to the left, and on the outside rather than on the inside of a page are seen and studied most often. The advertising positions selected by your competitors ought to be taken into account as well.

You then have to work out, either from the rate cards or by contacting the various advertisement departments, the respective costs of placing these advertisements within the remaining titles on your list. A precise 'value for money' comparison between each publication is difficult as their advertising rates will all differ according to circulation and readership figures, advertisement sizes and positions as well as discounts that are available for repeated advertising and at quiet times of the year. Nevertheless, making comparisons, rough and ready though they may be, is worthwhile so that those titles which seem to reach the correct type and number of customers at the best prices are kept and perhaps ranked in order of preference and those that appear to be less cost-effective are eliminated from your thoughts.

The traditional method of comparing prices – which can equally well be applied to different types of publications and advertisements – is to calculate the cost of reaching every thousand people within each title's circulation. Simply take the price of the advertisement (unit), dividing it by one-thousandth of the circulation to discover the 'cost per thousand'. As an example, one publication charges £3 per single column centimetre and has a 60,000 circulation. Its cost per thousand – £3 divided by 60 (60,000 divided by 1,000) – is 5 pence. Another title sells advertising space at £5 per single column centimetre and is circulated to 90,000 people. Its cost per thousand – £5 divided by 90 (90,000 divided by 1,000) – is 5.5 pence. Of course, the sensible advertiser recalls that high or low circulation, and therefore comparisons between publications solely on this basis, is less relevant than a title's readership and its profile in relation to and penetration into the target audience. Increasingly valid assessments may be made by appraising the cost of reaching every thousand readers *and* targeted customers.

Drafting your schedule

Having composed a list of potentially suitable titles, compared their audiences with your own, thought about the timing of your advertising activities and checked out the costs involved, you are now ready and able to pull together all of your knowledge and information and draft a provisional schedule for your press campaign. This should consist of the names of the newspapers, magazines and miscellaneous publications which you plan to use with their circulation, readership, profile and penetration figures and copy deadlines. Also include the number of advertisements within each title plus their sizes, positions, costs and insertion dates. Spell out the duration of your proposed campaign and the total estimated expenses which will be incurred.

Realistically, your first attempt at sketching out a schedule is unlikely to tally with your appropriation, more often than not substantially exceeding it. You should consider revising it by reducing or increasing the range of titles in which you might advertise, looking back over the publications that you have included to see if your audience will be fully contacted and whether certain sections might be excessively or inadequately covered. Consider cutting out those titles with profiles which do not match as well nor penetrate as far as others, in addition to those which largely address the same, identical people. Similarly, it would be wise to study the number of advertisements which you intend to place, making sure that all of your customers see them enough times for your message to be absorbed, but not so often that they become bored and ignore it.

You may choose to advertise on alternate days rather than every day to save money and decide to vary the layout and copy of advertisements to retain interest. See Chapter 8: 'Creating advertisements', page 60.

Contemplate taking smaller or larger advertisements, possibly in different positions within the newspapers, magazines and/or miscellaneous publications. You may be able to reduce the size and cost of your advertisements without detracting from the overall message – look at Chapter 8: 'Creating advertisements', page 60 – or you could relocate them on to other, less expensive pages whilst still being seen by the same, basic audience. It is sensible to reflect upon the duration of your planned campaign too, shortening or lengthening it, as relevant. Be wary of pumping money into more advertising once you have achieved your goals – check out Chapter 10: 'Conducting your activities', page 84. Going back over the preliminary schedule and its blend of key ingredients is a worthy and valid exercise. You will gain an increased awareness of the advertising mix and will – after several or even innumerable revisions – be able to match it to your appropriation. Filling in the 'Media schedule' form on page 59 may then be beneficial.

Summary

1. A prospective press advertiser and his or her advisers should work towards a campaign by tackling various tasks in sequence, namely:
   a) listing publications;
   b) comparing audiences;
   c) thinking about timing;
   d) checking out costs;
   e) drafting a schedule.

2. Listing publications involves several, separate steps. These are:
   a) setting down the types of publication that might be suitable in the circumstances, such as 'national dailies' and 'business magazines';
   b) obtaining details of actual titles within these categories – from BRAD and representative bodies in particular;
   c) requesting and subsequently studying closely media packs, rate cards and the latest editions of the respective titles.

3. It is essential that each publication's audience is compared alongside the target one. This involves:
   a) noting the key characteristics of the two audiences, side-by-side;
   b) analysing their profiles and how far the publication's audience penetrates into the target audience;

   c) ignoring the publication's circulation and readership figures – they are largely irrelevant unless they match the target audience.

4. Thinking about timing is important. It means:
   a) considering when to advertise;
   b) choosing how often to advertise;
   c) deciding how long to advertise for;
   d) assessing the copy deadlines of the various titles.

5. It is advisable to check out the costs of advertising in the different publications. Doing this involves:
   a) picking the sizes of advertisements;
   b) selecting the required positions for advertisements;
   c) calculating the costs of advertising in the numerous titles;
   d) comparing the costs in relation to each other, and the numbers of targeted customers reached.

6. The would-be advertiser and his or her advisers should then draft a schedule for the forthcoming press campaign. This means:
   a) outlining data about the chosen titles – circulation, readership, profile and penetration figures, plus copy deadlines;
   b) specifying the number of advertisements per title, as well as their sizes, positions, costs and insertion dates;
   c) recording the duration of the activities and total estimated expenditure;
   d) amending details as necessary to match the budget.

MEDIA SCHEDULE

Campaign:	Number:
Medium:	Date:

Medium \ Week beginning													

Media schedule form

8 Creating advertisements

WHETHER YOUR ADVERTISEMENTS are drawn up by you or composed on your behalf by advertising agency staff or other specialists in this field, you need to know more about the different types of advertisement that are available to you as well as how to choose an appropriate approach, decide upon the layout and select the correct copy for them. Despite the creativity involved in designing advertisements – which almost demands that you break suggested rules – a number of broad guidelines do exist that ought to be loosely adhered to. It is also sensible to find out about staying within the law when compiling your advertisements.

Types of advertisement

Without doubt, you already will have given some thought to display and classified advertisements whilst you were sketching down a schedule. See Chapter 1: 'Types of publication', page 1 and Chapter 7: 'Planning your schedule', page 50. Nevertheless, you now should pay further attention to these two alternatives and the particular advantages and disadvantages that they each offer to you, before going on to create or approve the approach, layout and copy of your own advertisements. You may even wish to amend your schedule in the light of your additional thoughts, consequently improving it.

A display advertisement – mixing perhaps a headline, illustration and text together inside its own borders – is distinctive and set apart from other, rival advertisements. With space for creative and design skills to be fully developed, it can be eye-catching and appealing to readers. In many instances, it may be placed on any page within a title – depending upon availability – thus ensuring that it is likely to be seen mostly by the right types and number of people. On the minus side, display advertising rates are usually relatively high and this could restrict the breadth and depth of your activities. Also, having more than sufficient room in which to work can be a drawback in the hands of an inexperienced or amateurish advertiser, serving simply to highlight his or her inadequacies and lack of imagination.

A classified advertisement, running on line by line beneath a heading such as 'Miscellaneous Sales' or 'Recruitment', is fairly inexpensive in comparison with displays. Only those dedicated readers who are especially interested in the field and whom you probably wish to address will scan through the classifieds, which normally are tucked away in the back pages of a title. Of course, there sometimes may be tens if not hundreds of classified advertisements to read, and yours could therefore be easier to overlook than to see, effectively wasting your money.

A semi-display advertisement is a display that is incorporated under a classified heading: 'Accountancy Services', 'Business Equipment' and so on. Such an advertisement, which is rarely considered as fully as it ought to be by advertisers, can combine the qualities of the two main types of advertisement. It may be attractive, separated from others around it, charged at a reasonable cost and looked at by readers who are keen to peruse it. At the same time, those negative aspects which are often attributed to display and classified advertisements can be avoided. Judging displays, classifieds and semi-displays alongside each other, you may decide to bring more semi-display advertisements into your schedule.

Choosing your approach

Many, varied approaches can be adopted towards advertisements, especially displays and semi-displays. Humour may be very effective if it is handled professionally. An amusing headline and/or illustration can draw readers' attention to an advertisement, whilst witty text may help to put across a message in a warm and friendly manner to people in a relaxed and therefore responsive mood. These advertisements can leave a lasting, memorable impression on readers long after they have turned the page and discarded the title. The Volvic advertisement on page 62 provides an excellent example of a humorous headline linked with an illustration. The Perrier and PC World advertisements on pages 63 and 64 highlights the clever use of word-plays, closely related to the products being sold by the advertisers.

In some instances, you may appeal to people's emotions – such as their ego, machismo, desire for status, paternal or maternal instincts and feelings of nostalgia – or could employ shock tactics to convey information. The Heinz and Blue Cross advertisements on pages 65 and 66 both play on the 'aah factor' amongst readers, to considerable effect. Those for the International League for the Protection of Horses, the League Against Cruel Sports and the National Society for the Prevention of Cruelty to Children on pages 67, 68 and 69 almost demand to be read and acted upon. In other situations, logic may prevail. The Kwik Save advertisements on pages 70 and 71 clearly set out the reasons why people ought to shop at *their* stores in preference to others.

This year, he's going to keep his Volvic on court.

Still, natural mineral water.

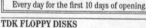

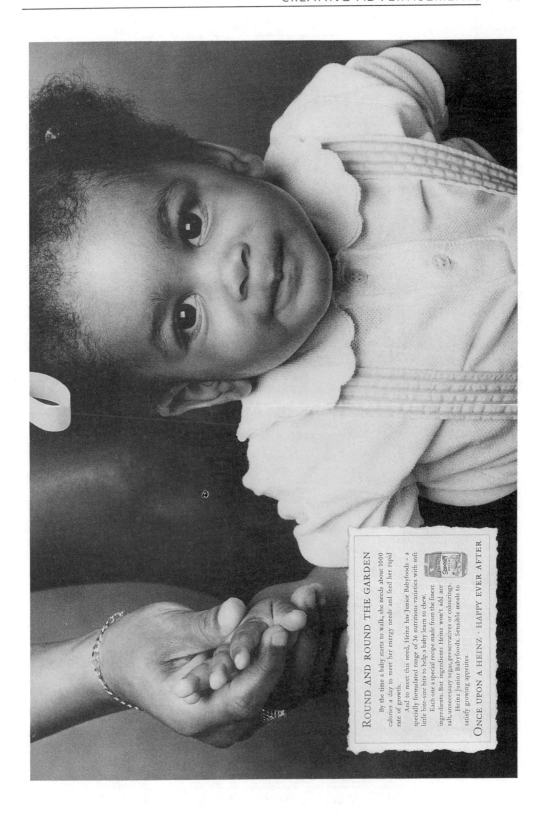

ROUND AND ROUND THE GARDEN

By the time a baby starts to walk, she needs about 1000 calories a day to meet her energy needs and feed her rapid rate of growth.

And to meet this need, Heinz has Junior Babyfoods – a specially formulated range of 36 nutritious varieties with soft little bite-size bits to help a baby learn to chew.

Each one a special recipe made from the finest ingredients. But ingredients Heinz won't add are salt, unnecessary sugar, preservatives or colourings.

Heinz Junior Babyfoods. Sensible meals to satisfy growing appetites.

ONCE UPON A HEINZ · HAPPY EVER AFTER

THE BLUE CROSS NEEDS YOU.

Every year the Blue Cross cares for thousands of animals, from kittens to horses.

Many are strays who not only need treatment but a loving home as well.

Others are brought to us for free treatment by owners who just can't afford vet fees.

And they all need you.

For the Blue Cross is a charity and relies solely on donations to survive.

So please help by filling in the coupon.

I enclose a cheque for £10 ☐ £20 ☐ £50 ☐ Other £_____
I'd like more information on The Blue Cross ☐

Name_____

Address_____

_____

_____ Postcode_____

To: The Blue Cross,
Room 54A, Shilton Road,
Burford, Oxon OX8 4PE   **BLUE✚CROSS**

If you can't look at the picture, please help us face the problem.

July 1990, Bari, S. Italy
A horse is winched up through the decks by its hind legs. It is still alive, but only just.
Its body, covered in wounds, was then dumped on the deck where it lay shaking until its death.
That was just one of 900 equines shipped from Argentina to Italy.
Five died en route, many others were injured.
This cruel, barbaric treatment of horses in transport is commonplace on the continent.
The ILPH is the largest international equine charity and we are fighting to stop it.
Please help us by lending your support now. **Thank you.**

I wish to lend my support by; Making a donation towards your 'General Fund' of £100☐, £50☐, £25☐, £10☐, OTHER☐. £5 of any donation will be used for your membership, or you may elect Life Membership (£50). Please send me your brochure.

Name_____

Address_____

Postcode _____ Signature_____

I enclose cheque/P.O. made payable to I.L.P.H., to the

sum of £_____ or please debit my Access/Visa/Amex card no. _____

☐☐☐☐☐☐☐☐☐☐☐☐☐☐☐☐☐

to the sum of £_____ Expiry date_____

I. L. P. H.
Founded 1927

REGISTERED CHARITY NO.206658.

INTERNATIONAL LEAGUE FOR THE PROTECTION OF HORSES

Dept.   , I.L.P.H. H.Q., Anne Colvin House, Snetterton, Norwich, Norfolk, NR16 2LR. Tel. 0953 498682

Fox-hunting is a sickening bloodsport.

Every year from November 1st, this horrific scene is repeated thousands of times across Britain.

Defenceless foxes run for their lives, chased by mounted hunters and 40 baying hounds.

When they are caught, they suffer a savage death.

Killed for fun.

The League Against Cruel Sports' campaign to ban this outrage is funded entirely by donations.

So if fox-hunting tears you apart, please part with as much as you can.

IF FOX-HUNTING TEARS YOU APART,

TEAR THIS OUT.

Yes, I want to help stop fox-hunting. You have my full support.

Please accept my donation of: £100 ☐ £50 ☐ £25 ☐ £15 ☐ Other £_____

(Please make cheques/postal orders payable to the League Against Cruel Sports)

Name (Mr/Mrs/Ms/Miss) _____

Address _____

_____

_____ Postcode _____

I wish to donate by Access/Visa

Card No. ☐☐☐☐☐☐☐☐☐☐☐☐☐☐☐☐☐

Expiry Date / /   Signature _____

LEAGUE
AGAINST CRUEL SPORTS

WORKING FOR WILDLIFE

Or phone our Hotline number on **071 378 6697** to make your credit card donation.

☐ Please send details of how I can make regular contributions by Standing Order.

☐ Please send more information about the League's campaigns to protect wildlife.

To: League Against Cruel Sports, Room 157 FREEPOST, 83-87 Union St, London SE1 1BT

DON'T LET BRITAIN'S WILDLIFE GO TO THE DOGS.

If you kept hearing the child next door screaming, is this how you'd stop it?

IT'S THAT NOISE again. The same one that you heard last night, and two nights ago.

It sounds like a child screaming, but you'd rather not think about it. So you turn the TV up, or do the hoovering. Anything to blot it out.

No matter what you do though, it doesn't stop you thinking. Countless thoughts race through your mind.

You try to persuade yourself it's something else. A hungry cat for instance. Or a whistling kettle.

And even if it is the child, he's probably a right little handful, and deserves to be taught a lesson.

Though he doesn't seem like a naughty kid. Maybe he is being ill-treated. But it's nothing to do with you what people get up to in their own houses, is it?

The fact of the matter is, it is your business. You could be the child's only chance of being saved from the horrors of physical abuse. Ignoring the screams can't stop the child's suffering. Calling the NSPCC Child Protection Helpline can.

We realise reporting a neighbour is a difficult decision to make. But don't be put off by thinking that you'll split up the family. Children only get taken into care in very few cases.

When a case is reported to us, first we listen closely to what is said and then decide on the best course of action.

An NSPCC Child Protection Officer or Local Authority social worker may then visit the child's home.

After this, we then make a careful assessment of the family to identify why the parents have been mistreating their child. In a lot of cases, they don't even realise they've been doing wrong. A period of counselling may then follow which can often involve helping the parents learn how to love and understand their children.

We always prefer it if you give your name, but the most important thing to us is to stop a child being at further risk from abuse.

Maybe you think it can't be going on next door to you. But unfortunately, that's what most people think.

Reporting a case isn't the only way you can help, however. We're always crying out for donations. 80% of our funding relies on the generosity of the public.

And please remember, if you keep hearing a child scream, picking up the TV remote control can't stop it. Picking up the phone can.

For further information on the work of the NSPCC, or to make a donation, write to: NSPCC, 67 Saffron Hill, London, EC1N 8RS or call 071-242 1626.

To report a suspected case of abuse, call the NSPCC Child Protection Helpline on 0800 800 500.

NSPCC
Act Now For Children.

LOOK AT THESE SAVINGS -AND SEE HOW LOW YOUR SHOPPING BILL CAN GO.

In a price survey carried out on 14th November, the following items were purchased from Budgens, Milton Keynes and Kwik Save, Dunstable. The columns below show how much less was paid by shopping at Kwik Save compared with Budgens.

	KWIK SAVE	BUDGENS	YOU SAVE
ST. IVEL GOLD 250gm	38p	39p	1p
LURPAK Butter 250gm	68p	69p	1p
MR KIPLING 6 Apple Pies	79p	£1.03	24p
GOLDEN SHRED Marmalade 454gm	69p	72p	3p
HELLMANS Mayonnaise 400gm	£1.09	£1.13	4p
KIT KAT 7 pack	57p	61p	4p
WALKERS Handy Size Crisps 30gm	18p	21p	3p
COCA COLA 330ml can	24p	26p	2p
CHUNKY Dog Food Large 412gm	31p	32p	1p
McVITIES Digestive Biscuits 400gm	49p	51p	2p
McVITIES Penguin 7 pack	55p	58p	3p
COMFORT Fabric Conditioner 1 ltr	89p	91p	2p
ANDREX Toilet Rolls 4 pack	£1.52	£1.56	4p
MIGHTY WHITE Sliced Loaf 800gm	54p	61p	7p
CADBURYS Dairy Milk 200gm	79p	82p	3p
HEINZ Sponge Pudding 300gm	66p	72p	6p
POLO MINTS 5 pack	49p	53p	4p
SMARTIES 3 pack	55p	65p	10p
CADBURYS Twirl 5 pack	53p	55p	2p

*Own label/specially packed for Budgens

	KWIK SAVE	BUDGENS	YOU SAVE
MARS BARS Snack Size 8 pack	£1.05	£1.25	20p
CELEBRITY/OLDE OAK Round Ham 454gm	85p	95p PRINCES	10p
UNCLE BENS Stir Fry Sauce 350gm	95p	99p	4p
TOLLY BOY/WHITWORTHS Long Grain Rice 1kg	79p	£1.19 TILDA	40p
TYPHOO QT Instant White Tea 150gm	£1.25	£1.29	4p
CADBURYS/ROWNTREES Cocoa 125gm	65p	78p	13p
TETLEY Tea Bags 240 pack	£4.47	£4.55	8p
LYONS Original Ground Coffee 227gm	£1.25	£1.39	14p
PRINCES Spaghetti in Tomato Sauce 411gm	21p	*26p (440gm)	5p
Q-MATIC Automatic Liquid 2 ltr	£1.97	*£2.75	78p
PAMPERS Disposable Nappies all sizes	£6.15	£8.49	£2.34
ROSS Value Garden Peas 2 lbs	47p	*69p	22p
PERRIER Water 75cl	57p	59p	2p
JACOBS Club 6 pack	49p	56p	7p
ROWNTREES Jelly assorted 1 pint	26p	29p	3p
HORLICKS Instant Low Fat 500gm	£1.89	£1.95	6p
TYPHOO Tea 125gm	67p	70p	3p
NESCAFÉ 200gm	£2.63	£2.69	6p
MARS Ice Cream Bars 4 pack	£1.89	£1.99	10p

CHAMPION PRICE FIGHTERS

As well as our usual top brands, we have selected a range of quality products that we are able to offer at exceptionally low prices – even by our standards.

SHOPPER'S CHAMPION

KWIK SAVE

NO NONSENSE/FOODSTORES

Kwik Save's policy is to offer the best value shopping basket in town. Due to localised 'price wars,' prices on products shown above may therefore be lower in certain Kwik Save stores.

NOW CELEBRATING OUR 750th STORE OPENING

COMPARE THESE PRICES

BUDGENS

KELLOGGS Cornflakes 500gm	£1.15
WEETABIX 24 pack	94p
PG TIPS 160 Tea Bags	£3.15
PASTEURISED MILK 4 Pts	£1.09
GRANULATED SUGAR 1 kg	66p
TIZER 2 Ltr	91p
DOLMIO 475gm	£1.18
BUDGENS Baked Beans 440gm	27p
McVITIES Milk Chocolate Homewheat 300gm	74p
McVITIES Cheddars 150gm	43p
PHILADELPHIA 200gm	£1.12
BUDGENS Pink Salmon 213gm	82p
SKI Fruit Yoghurt x1	28p
WHITE SLICED LOAF	49p
GOLDEN WONDER Pot Noodle	69p

TOTAL £13.92

KWIK SAVE

KELLOGGS Cornflakes 500gm	92p
WEETABIX 24 pack	83p
PG TIPS 160 Tea Bags	£3.09
PASTEURISED MILK 4 Pts	98p
GRANULATED SUGAR 1 kg	59p
TIZER 2 Ltr	82p
DOLMIO 475gm	£1.09
PRINCES Baked Beans 425gm	17p
McVITIES Milk Chocolate Homewheat 300gm	69p
McVITIES Cheddars 150gm	36p
PHILADELPHIA 200gm	89p
JOHN WEST/PRINCES Pink Salmon 213gm	53p
SKI Fruit Yoghurt x1	26p
WHITE SLICED LOAF	29p
GOLDEN WONDER Pot Noodle	65p

TOTAL £12.16

AT THE END OF THE DAY YOU'LL APPRECIATE WHY OUR STORES HAVE NO FRILLS

OUR CHARTER

For over 25 years Kwik Save's charter has been to bring you Britain's favourite brands at Britain's favourite prices.

We've done so by sticking with some basic business beliefs from which over 4 million customers a week now benefit at 750 stores.

BELIEF 1
The more efficiently we operate, the more you benefit from the best prices.

BELIEF 2
We only sell top brands and top sellers, and never compromise on quality.

BELIEF 3
We will always use our buying power to keep costs to a minimum, and pass on the savings through our everyday low prices.

BELIEF 4
We will operate smaller, efficient stores that are easy to shop at and easy to get to.

BELIEF 5
We will not insult you with frills or gimmicks that you the customer end up paying for.

We believe that all this adds up to the best value grocery shopping in the country.

SHOPPER'S CHAMPION

"I've been shopping at Kwik Save for about six years now. The prices are cheaper than at other stores and there's plenty of choice. It's perfect for me and my family"

Mrs. K. Lewis

"We prefer brands we know and at Kwik Save we can get them cheaper than anywhere else"

Mr & Mrs Baker

KWIK SAVE

NO NONSENSE FOODSTORES

NOW CELEBRATING OUR 750th STORE OPENING

Incorporating a well-known personality into an advertisement with his or her permission – whether a local or national celebrity, cartoon or puppet character or a renowned expert in the field – gives status and adds credibility to your firm, goods and services, and can remind readers of you when he or she (or it) are seen elsewhere, possibly on television. Demonstrating a product – its appearance, in action or the results of using it – may be extremely effective, particularly if colour is available to you. Kodak's advertisement on page 73 cleverly combines two approaches – the use of a famous face and a demonstration of the quality of their product. Sometimes, comparisons are made between one company and its rivals, in terms of the respective strengths, weaknesses and so on. Those Kwik Save advertisements on pages 70 and 71 adopt this technique, with some strength.

Of course, the approach which you select – whether using humour, emotion, logic, a personality, demonstration, comparison or a combination – must depend upon your own individual situation. You have to compare and contrast the numerous approaches alongside your business, goods and services, goals, customers, competitors, market and budget. One or more techniques may stand out as being potentially ideal for you, whilst others could be obviously unsuitable in the circumstances. Your concern – perhaps a funeral parlour – may be ill-suited to humour, but well matched with emotion. Your products could need to be demonstrated – the tanning effects of a sun lotion – to maximize their benefits. Possibly your budget, limited by a poor cash flow, does not stretch to commissioning a personality, which may run into hundreds or even thousands of pounds for a nationally known face.

Deciding upon layout

Aware of the types of advertisement and the approach that you will be using, you then have to consider exactly what your advertising message will be. Naturally, this will be tied in with your forthcoming goals – perhaps you will decide to stress the key consumer benefits of your product if you are trying to increase sales, possibly you will promote the advantages of shopping by post if you are seeking to sell goods direct to customers, and so on. (Never forget that customers want to know what's in it for them.) Although advertisements may vary slightly – from one region to another, to test them and so forth – the same basic message ought to run throughout the campaign or at least until the objective has been achieved, constantly hammering home the points that you are attempting to make. It should be reflected in and supported by the headline, illustration and text which make up the layout of your display and semi-display advertisements.

Your headline is vitally important, hopefully catching the readers' attention and sparking off sufficient interest to make them study all of the

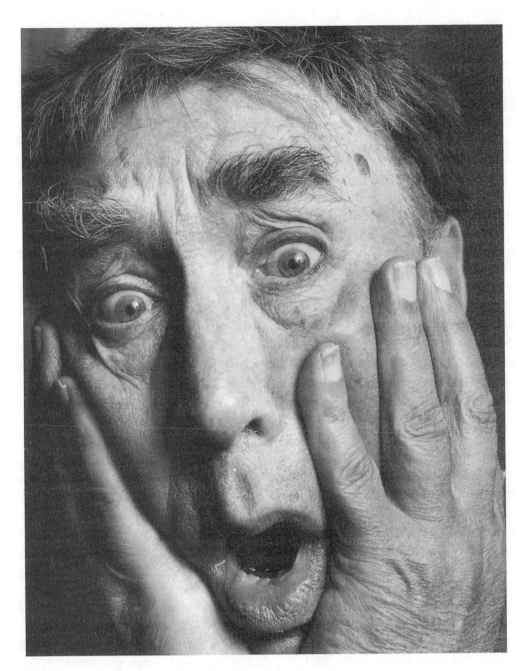

EKTAR RESOLUTION: A FRANK EXPOSÉ.

 When you've tittered as much as Frankie Howerd, you can expect a few laughter lines. As is revealed by the candid sharpness of EKTAR film.

Whether you choose 25, 125 or 1000 speed, Kodak EKTAR film will give you superbly clear enlargements.

This is because it has 'T' Grain technology, tabular shaped grains in the emulsion that catch the light more effectively. Resulting in photographs that are visibly more detailed and virtually grain-free.

Though not, unfortunately for Frankie, wrinkle-free.

TOO SHARP FOR SOME.

advertisement and take in its message. You need to ask yourself what heading will force your target customers to stop, concentrate and read carefully. You may choose a headline that is interrogative (see the National Society for the Prevention of Cruelty to Children advertisement on page 69), dramatic (see the International League for the Protection of Horses advertisement on page 67), declarative (refer to the League Against Cruel Sports advertisement on page 68) or humorous (look at the PC World advertisement on page 64), according to your situation. Whatever you decide to put – such as the job title for a recruitment advertisement, the discounts offered for a closing down sale advertisement and so on – it should encapsulate and sum up the main thrust of your message in one succinct word, phrase or line, as these examples do.

An illustration – whether a sketch, photograph or cartoon supplied by a specialist – can also serve to capture and retain readers' thoughts, complementing or sometimes even replacing the headline. You must question which picture will be looked at by your audience and will convey and strengthen your advertising message. The illustrative material used ought to be simple, relevant and self-explanatory; see the Blue Cross advertisement on page 66 which is clear, to the point and cries out 'Help Me!' at first sight. The other illustrated examples, especially those of the International League for the Protection of Horses and the League Against Cruel Sports, are equally effective. A busy or obscure drawing or photograph will succeed only in blurring and detracting from what you are trying to say.

The appearance of the text – whether ten or 100 words – can be attractive or unappealing, persuading or dissuading people from reading the advertisement. You may choose from a number of type designs – or 'faces' as they are more widely known – which should build on or could lessen the impact of your advertisement. For example, to further put across the image of a long-established, traditional family business in order to uphold its reputation you might pick a fitting, old-fashioned typeface. Other, popular tricks of the trade include varying the shades of the faces, alternating bold typefaces with italics and having white faces on a black background. A range of typefaces have been used in the PC World and other advertisements, and these should be studied. Whatever you choose, make sure that it is both appealing and easy to read.

You have to think about how to lay out the headline, illustration and text in the most attractive way. By studying all of the examples on pages 62 to 73, you can see that there are no hard and fast rules. Headlines are at the top of the advertisements, halfway down, below photographs or even replaced by them. Different types of illustration are used in various places and text is scattered from left to right and from top to bottom. It is wise to discuss your ideas with your commissioned specialists who are there to advise you. Alternatively, you may be offered help by the production department of the titles in which you will advertise, depending on whether they have the time and inclination to do so. You may be fortunate to find a guardian angel, although this is often the exception rather than the rule.

Selecting copy

Not surprisingly, you need to think further about the words, phrases and expressions you are going to put into advertisements. As a rule, copy should be clear and to the point, using everyday words in simple sentences and short paragraphs – like those in the Blue Cross and the League Against Cruel Sports advertisements on pages 66 and 68. Relatively few readers will take in complex ideas and detailed explanations. Generally, avoid lengthy text, however clearly written it may be. Unnecessary words and sentences can obscure the sales message. Even the fuller PC World and Kwik Save advertisements on pages 64 and 70–71 are still brief and direct, and easy to absorb.

Often, it is sensible to set out copy in a logical order, perhaps stressing the one key benefit so far as the reader is concerned, or several selling points in turn. Take another look at that Kodak advertisement on page 73, noting the main benefit that it is emphasizing over and again to great effect. Similarly, the Kwik Save advertisements on pages 70 and 71 are equally effective, if not more so, really driving home to the reader what's in it for them. Constantly repeating the same basic message: 'It's sharper!', 'We're cheaper!' or whatever, is a successful tactic, helping to lodge it in the back of the reader's mind.

Hopefully, your advertisements will be stylish and distinctive, and the copy can enable you to achieve this. Make sure it flows and is readable, paying attention to grammar, spelling and punctuation. See the National Society for the Prevention of Cruelty to Children advertisement on page 69 as a good example of this. Try to be original, steering away from clichés, corny expressions and trite phrases. Sound positive and enthusiastic, to encourage the reader to act now, otherwise the moment will pass and they will move on to the next page of the newspaper, magazine or miscellaneous publication. That NSPCC advertisement attempts to achieve this, in a variety of ways.

Staying within the law

It is essential that your advertisements comply with the laws of the land and the British Code of Advertising Practice, which is the advertising industry's self-regulatory control system. Those advertisements which fail to reach acceptable standards will not be taken by reputable publications. The Advertising Standards Authority and the Committee of Advertising Practice also regularly monitor and deal with complaints about press advertising, seeking to have offending advertisements changed, withdrawn or dropped, if necessary. Look at Appendix C: 'The British Code of Advertising Practice', page 131.

To adhere to the Code, you need to check back to ensure that your advertisements are: legal, with their contents neither breaching the law, bringing it into disrepute nor omitting anything which needs to be incorporated within them; decent, by not including any matter which might cause grave or widespread distaste or offence; honest, by not exploiting consumers' vulnerabilities such as a lack of knowledge or experience and by making certain that the advertising message and any points which are made are easy to grasp and understand; and truthful, by not trying to mislead consumers through inaccuracies, ambiguities, exaggerations or omissions.

Advertisements then have to be prepared with a sense of responsibility to consumers and society. Thus, they must not: play on fear nor excite distress without good cause; condone nor incite violence or anti-social behaviour; portray or refer to any living person unless prior permission has been obtained from them; cause offence to those connected in any way with deceased persons depicted or referred to; show or advocate dangerous behaviour or unsafe practices unless in the context of promoting safety; or contain anything which may lead to physical, mental or moral harm to children or might exploit their credulity, lack of experience or sense of loyalty.

You should further make sure that your advertisements conform to the principles of fair competition which are generally accepted in business. Hence: comparisons ought to deal fairly with rivals and be set out in such a way that there is no likelihood of a consumer being misled on any matter; competitors' products should not be described or shown to be broken, defaced, inoperative or ineffective, nor discredited by any other unfair means; inaccurate or irrelevant comments concerning the persons, characters or actions of rivals ought to be excluded; and advertisements should not resemble others to a degree whereby they might mislead or confuse. If or when your advertisements meet *all* of these terms and conditions, you are ready to move on to purchase advertising spaces.

Summary

1. Would-be press advertisers may create their own advertisements, or employ others to do it for them. Whatever their preference, they need to know about:
   a) the types of advertisement available;
   b) choosing an appropriate approach;
   c) deciding upon layout;

d) selecting the copy;
e) staying within the law.

2. Several types of advertisement exist, each with their own advantages and disadvantages. These are:
   a) display advertisements;
   b) classified advertisements;
   c) semi-display advertisements.

3. Many, varied approaches can be adopted towards advertisements, including those which are:
   a) humorous;
   b) emotional;
   c) logical;
   d) personality based;
   e) demonstrative;
   f) comparative.

4. The layout of advertisements should be linked to the message that is being put across. Attention must be given in particular to:
   a) the headline;
   b) the illustrations, if appropriate;
   c) the text.

5. The contents of advertisements is equally important. Copy should be:
   a) clear and to the point;
   b) logical;
   c) stylish and distinctive.

6. All advertisements in the press must comply with the British Code of Advertising Practice. This means they have to be:
   a) legal;
   b) decent;
   c) honest;
   d) truthful;
   e) prepared with a sense of responsibility to consumers and society;
   f) fair to competitors.

9 Buying advertising space

WHETHER YOU PLAN to manage your advertising campaign your-self or have decided to delegate responsibilities and tasks to a full service agency or a media independent, you should know how to purchase spaces within the newspapers, magazines and miscellaneous publications which you have chosen to use. It is important that you can read a rate card prop-erly and are able to negotiate with the representatives who have been sent along by advertisement managers, subsequently dealing with the various titles in a correct and efficient manner. Only then can you hope to be successfully involved with advertising activities in this medium.

Reading the rate card

The rate card which lists advertising costs and other relevant data about a title is the basis for your discussions with representatives and publications. It is wise to be aware of the trade jargon used within it, perhaps concerning the type and size of advertisements. Some words and phrases will already be famil-iar to you, namely 'display', 'classified' and 'semi-display' advertisements, 'linage', single column centimetre' or 'SCC' and 'double-page spread' or 'DPS'. Others are self-explanatory, including 'quarter', 'half', 'whole' and 'full-page'. A number will be unknown to you though. An 'advertorial' is a promotional fea-ture that accompanies an advertisement. An 'insert' is an advertising item such as a leaflet which is loosely placed within or bound into a publication. A 'gate-fold' is a sheet with folded-in leaves. The 'type area' is the part of the page taken up with editorial and advertising matter. 'Bleed off' means extending an adver-tisement off the edge of a page for maximum impact.

You also need to be able to recognize the different terms which relate to the positioning of advertisements. 'Inside front cover' or 'IFC', 'first left-hand page' or 'first LHP', 'first right-hand page' or 'first RHP', 'inside back cover' or 'IBC' and 'outside back cover' or 'OBC' are all self-evident. Others are less obvi-ous. 'Title cover', 'ear', 'ear pieces' or 'ear specs' refer to the spaces to the sides of the front page title. 'Run of paper', 'run of press' or 'ROP' indicate that adver-tisements will be located anywhere in the publication at the publisher's discretion. 'Run of week', 'run of month' and 'run of year' – 'ROW', 'ROM', and 'ROY' respectively – mean that advertisements will be printed at a date selected by the publisher. A 'special position' guarantees a certain space for an advertisement, as chosen by the advertiser. A 'solus position' ensures that an advertisement is the only one on the page. An 'island position' indicates that an advertisement will be surrounded by editorial text. 'Facing matter' or 'FM' and 'next matter' or 'NM' mean that advertisements will be sited facing or next to editorial copy.

The remaining jargon is usually associated with technical and mechanical data which will normally not concern you, as either specialists or, more likely, the publications themselves will handle the production of your advertisements. Nevertheless, it is sensible to be conscious of the most frequently used language on the card. 'Mono' means black and white with 'spot colour' or 'single spot' referring to a colour which may be added to highlight parts of an advertisement. 'Colour' suggests that a full range of varied colours is available to enhance advertisements, albeit of mixed quality in newspapers and some miscellaneous publications. 'Copy' usually relates to the text of an advertisement, although the word often encompasses 'artwork' too, which describes illustrative matter such as drawings and photographs. 'Camera ready' means that copy is ready to be passed to the production department. A 'block' is a plate with an illustration etched onto it and is used during printing. A 'bromide' is a photographic print on bromide paper. 'Letterpress', 'litho' and 'gravure' are different printing methods.

The terms and conditions of acceptance of advertisements are printed on the reverse (or at the back) of the rate card. You ought to carefully study these before tackling representatives and publications. Although the order and phrasing of clauses may vary from one card to another, their contents are very similar, if not identical in many instances. Expect to see statements such as: 'all advertisements must conform to the Consumer Credit Act of 1974, the Sex Discrimination Act of 1975, the Business Advertisements (Disclosure) Order of 1977, the Trade Descriptions Act of 1986 and the British Code of Advertising Practice; orders have to be confirmed in writing no later than so many days or weeks before the publication; artwork and other material must be submitted so many days or weeks ahead of publication; the publisher cannot be held responsible for the loss of or damage to the advertiser's property.'

Also: 'the publisher reserves the right to refuse, amend or withdraw advertisements even if previously accepted and paid for; cancellations have to be notified in writing no less than so many days or weeks prior to publication; the advertiser must check and return 'proofs' – copies of (parts of) pages – no later than so many days or weeks before publication. No changes may be made at this stage except to correct spelling and grammatical mistakes and facts which differ from the advertiser's original copy; the publisher is not liable for any loss or damage resulting from a failure to publish or distribute the title; if omissions, errors or misprints occur which materially affect advertisements, the publisher shall either adjust the cost, provide a reasonable refund up to the price of the advertising space or reinsert the advertisements at a later date. All omissions, errors and misprints must be notified to the publisher in writing within so many days of publication; payment has to be made with the initial order/on receipt of the invoice/on receipt of the monthly statement; voucher copies – complimentary issues of a title – are available upon written request by the advertiser.'

Negotiating with representatives

Having studied numerous rate cards in some detail, you now should be ready to meet representatives of the publications in which you want to advertise. The representatives of chosen titles will normally visit you at your shop, office or factory within a day or so of your telephone calls, and are worth talking to in depth. If they are good at their work, they will know all about their publications and may offer general and specific guidance concerning schedules, advertisements and the do's and don't's of space buying for the particular titles. The representatives act as hands-on sources of information and advice, and work as intermediaries between you and the departments which exist in their newspapers, magazines and/or miscellaneous publications.

When meeting a representative for the first time, probably on an informal basis during a coffee or tea break, you ought to seize the opportunity to learn as much as possible from him or her. You should ask about the title, seeking to confirm and expand (or perhaps adjust) your understanding of its characteristics, departments, staff and workings, circulation, readership and advertising rates, production methods and capabilities, rival media and their strengths or weaknesses plus its relationships with advertisers. Similarly, a representative who is dedicated to doing his or her job properly – by selling only the type, size and amount of space which is suitable for you – will question you about your firm, products and services, goals, customers, competitors, market and proposed budget. From your answers, he or she should be able to study and comment upon the viability of your planned schedule and its timing, frequency, duration and so on as well as your advertisements and their approaches, layouts and copy.

Establishing a rapport with representatives who carry out their duties in a conscientious and thorough manner, you ought to listen to their knowledgeable (albeit biased) opinions, amending your schedule and/or advertisements accordingly. It is then tempting to book, and even pay for, all advertisements for the forthcoming quarter, six months or year, especially as discounts of up to 20 per cent may be readily offered or made available on demand. Whatever deals can be negotiated – and you should always push hard for price reductions for first-time orders, for series of advertisements, at quiet times and for payments in advance – only make verbal bookings for the initial few insertions with remaining ones being pencilled in by both parties. It is sensible to continue to adopt a measured, step-by-step strategy to advertising, testing your ideas, spotting flaws and rectifying mistakes at an early stage before committing yourself to long-term expenditure. Refer to Chapter 10: 'Conducting your activities', page 84.

Dealing with publications

Your opening orders with the various titles must be confirmed in writing as soon as possible after your meetings with the representatives, and certainly before the deadlines imposed in the respective rate cards. Addressing your letters to the Classified or Display Advertisement Managers – unless representatives are acting as go-betweens for you and the different departments – you should simply state the advertisement sizes, positions, dates, agreed costs and discount terms and conditions. Follow this correspondence by sending in your copy, illustrations and photographs for the advertisements, if not already taken by the representatives. Ensure that they arrive in good time – delivering them in person if necessary – particularly if advertisement and production staff need to work on them on your behalf prior to publication. Retain the originals or satisfactory copies in case your submitted material is lost, which occasionally happens in busy and chaotic offices.

Some titles will automatically supply you with the proofs of your advertisements ahead of publication although others will need to be asked well in advance to forward them to you. Always request, obtain and look at them, making certain that the advertisement and production teams have interpreted your thoughts and suggestions properly, any changes which may have been made meet with your approval and advertisements are free of typographical and factual errors. Although amendments at this stage are expensive for the publication, you should not hesitate to notify them of mistakes which are their or the printer's responsibility. Left uncorrected, those flawed advertisements could reflect badly on you and may obscure or detract from your advertising message.

On publication, copies of each of the titles which carried your advertisements ought to be posted or brought to you by the representatives, but may have to be requested if the publications are poorly organized or the representatives are half-hearted at their work. Time-consuming though it is, carefully check to see that the advertisements were the right sizes (half, not quarter pages and so on), in the correct positions (displays not semi-displays and so forth) and were printed on the appropriate days or at satisfactory times if booked as run of week or run of month. Assess their overall appearance (quality of reproduction, enlargement, reduction and so on) and the positive and negative features of the surrounding material (the appeal of editorial copy, presence of rivals' advertisements etc.).

You must immediately contact the appropriate titles if any errors have occurred and/or you have genuine grievances, negotiating costs and/or seeking refunds. Read through invoices submitted to you, ensuring that they relate to the correct advertisements, that costs and discounts are duly noted and agreed payment terms and conditions are incorporated within them. Always pay promptly to maintain good relations. Based on your experiences so far – of the representatives, publications and their treatment of you and your advertisements – you may choose to cancel some subsequent bookings, giving the required notice in writing and rearranging your schedule as necessary. Look at Chapter 10: 'Conducting your activities', page 84.

Summary

1. A potential press advertiser and his or her advisers should set about buying advertising space by conducting activities in three, key stages:
   a) reading the rate card;
   b) negotiating with representatives;
   c) dealing with publications.

2. The rate card forms the basis of discussions with representatives and publications. It specifies data about:
   a) the types and sizes of advertisements;
   b) the positions of advertisements;
   c) technical and mechanical facts;
   d) the terms and conditions of acceptance of advertisements.

3. Negotiations with representatives should take place face-to-face on home territory. They involve:
   a) learning as much as possible about the publication;
   b) providing background information about the firm, products, services, goals, customers, competitors, market and budget;
   c) discussing, and perhaps amending, the schedule and proposed advertisements;
   d) making provisional, test bookings, preferably at discounted rates.

4. Dealing with publications consists of various tasks, more specifically:
   a) confirming test bookings and details in writing;
   b) sending in copy in good time;
   c) checking proofs are correct, and making amendments, if necessary;
   d) obtaining copies of the publications when available, and perusing them;
   e) checking invoices upon receipt, and querying them, if relevant;
   f) confirming or cancelling subsequent bookings, as appropriate.

10 Conducting your activities

OPERATING YOUR ADVERTISING CAMPAIGN alone, you must know how to administer a trial run to test and assess the success of your activities, monitoring responses and making changes to your planned schedule and advertisements to maximize your chances of future rewards. Even if you are overseeing the work of outside specialists such as an advertising agency or a media independent, it is sensible to be conversant with what and what not to do so that you are able to appraise how well the campaign is being managed on your behalf.

Administering a trial run

You need to step back and contemplate the opening stages of your schedule and the early advertisements. You have to find out if you are moving along the right lines before spending any more of your advertising appropriation. It is wise to prepare for this tricky and sometimes almost impossible assessment by setting questions about the make-up of your schedule which you will subsequently attempt to answer. In particular, you will want to try to discover whether suitable publications are being used and if appropriately sized advertisements are being well located and published at relevant times.

Also, you should list assorted questions concerning the component parts of your various advertisements. Typically, you will wish to find out whether you are choosing the right kinds of advertisement in this instance and if your selected approach is fitting in the circumstances. Then, your thoughts ought to turn to the layout and contents of your advertisements, seeking to ascertain whether they are appropriate or not. If they are not, they may be having little or even no impact, thus wasting your funds.

You also need to attempt to judge how far and how well the opening part of your schedule and initial batch of advertisements are helping you to fulfil your objectives. Depending on your various goals, you may be wondering whether independent retailers and consumers in the county are beginning to become aware of your new goods and their benefits, if a contacts list of potential retail stockists is starting to be built up and whether you are generating the targeted turnover.

Monitoring responses

In order to appraise the quality of your schedule and advertisements and how they are helping you to achieve your goals, you must monitor the responses to each of your advertisements. You need to evaluate the enquiries received if you are trying to develop a contacts list, build up a customer base or recruit staff. It is necessary to measure sales should you be attempting to sell direct, adjust demand, generate turnover or clear out stock. You have to assess changing moods and opinions if you are seeking to increase product recognition, reassure, remind or notify developments to customers or uphold the firm's reputation.

Evaluating the enquiries which derive from individual advertisements is a relatively straightforward process. You can ascertain which advertisement initiated a response by inserting a different 'key', or identifying mark, into each of your advertisements. You might ask readers to write to varied addresses (20–30 Windmill Road may become 20a, 20b, 21a, 21b onwards), departments, desks or rooms (Department SE for the *Sunday Express*, SE1 for the first advertisement in that paper, and so on) or people (Sophie Louise Jones could be Ms S. Jones, Ms S. L. Jones, S. Jones and other variations). Alternatively, you may suggest that they quote a reference number when corresponding with or telephoning you, perhaps NW3A for the advertisement which appeared in the *News of the World* on 3 April. Responses can then be logged alongside the appropriate advertisements.

Often, you can measure sales in the same manner, simply noting down addresses on letters, references on orders and so forth, and matching them to the advertisements in which they originally appeared. Naturally, this task has to be tackled carefully, especially if sales do not immediately arise but are spread out over several months following the advertisement, and perhaps after initial enquiries too. If orders are not sent direct to you, sales and the effects of your schedule and advertisements upon them may be harder to judge. You could need to conduct audits of opening stock levels, plus/minus deliveries and closing stock levels at distribution and retail outlets, comparing figures with previous periods whilst making allowances for different and ever-changing internal and external scenarios.

In many instances when you are evaluating enquiries and measuring sales, you can make further value-for-money assessments between advertisements, similar to those which you made when you selected the titles to go into your schedule. Dividing the price of an advertisement by the number of enquiries received from it gives you a comparable cost-per-enquiry figure. Similarly, if you divide the cost of the advertisement by the quantity of sales generated by it, you will be left with a cost-per-sale figure. Clearly, you must also bear in mind the number of enquiries which turn into sales and the amounts of each sale before reaching any firm conclusions.

Assessing developing moods and opinions – possibly of stockists and/or consumers – is extremely difficult as they cannot be quantified in terms of the number of enquiries or orders, although those who do enquire or order goods could be considered to have been reminded and reassured of products and services. You – or more likely specialists such as a full service agency or market research company – have to interview customers (or whoever you are trying to influence) before and after advertisements have been published, questioning them about their knowledge of the firm, goods and services plus their opinions on any recent changes that you have implemented. Questions could also be raised about their purchase and usage of products to further measure or check upon estimated sales.

Knowing about the enquiries, sales and changes of opinion which are attributable to each keyed advertisement may now enable you to answer some of the questions that you posed about your early schedule and advertisements. Perhaps advertisements in one title produced far fewer responses than those in others. Possibly, advertisements with a particular mix of contents did far better than other ones. Of course, you cannot expect to answer every query as fully as you would wish to, given the modest amount of advertising carried out so far. Nevertheless, you should be able to put together a rough and ready impression of what seems to work, and not to work. Take a look at the 'Media assessment' form on page 87 at this point. It may assist you in your activities.

Making changes

Mindful of your initial impressions, you should then set about revising your schedule and advertisements accordingly, dropping one or two titles that failed to generate any replies, concentrating on display rather than semi-display advertisements, shifting your approach and so on. You may decide to cancel several outstanding insertions which have been booked, if you are sure that they are unlikely to stimulate the number and type of responses which you are seeking. Make certain you adhere to the cancellation terms and conditions on the individual rate cards.

It is imperative that you continue with your advertising activities step by step, possibly placing one month's advertisements at a time. Always be conscious that your early opinions cannot be complete and may even be inaccurate on occasions. You could have deduced that one advertisement initiates more responses than another, does better in this rather than that title and on one particular day compared to others; but never forget that you are working on limited data. Don't be in too much of a hurry to hand over your money until you have a more substantial body of evidence and have filled in any gaps in your knowledge, perhaps about frequency and duration.

MEDIA ASSESSMENT FORM

Campaign: Number:

Medium	Cost incurred (£)	Number of enquiries	Cost per enquiry (£)	Number of orders	Cost per order (£)	Total sales	Average sale per enquiry (£)	Average sale per order (£)	Comment

Medium: Date:

Completed by: Signature: Checked by: Signature:

Media assessment form

Also, internal and external factors can alter as time passes. Internally, your business may contract or expand, with differing strengths and weaknesses becoming apparent. Products and services could come and go. You might amend your short-, medium- and long-term goals. Externally, new customers and rivals may come into the market, as others leave. Political, social and other influences could affect your marketplace, for better or for worse. These developments can all have knock-on effects upon your campaign. Hence, you need to pursue a hands-on approach at all times, analysing yourself, your market, schedule, advertisements and their results over and again, never being afraid to make amendments as required, even to long-held practices.

Summary

1. Those press advertisers who plan their advertising activities are most likely to conduct a successful campaign. To ensure this, they should:
   a)   administer a trial run;
   b)   monitor responses;
   c)   make changes, as appropriate.

2. Administering a trial run means asking and answering questions about:
   a)   the use of different publications;
   a)   all aspects of the advertisements;
   c)   how far the schedule and advertisements are helping to fulfil objectives.

3. Responses need to be monitored on a careful and thorough basis. It involves:
   a)   evaluating enquiries and sales through the use of identifying marks in advertisements;
   b)   subsequently making value-for-money assessments;
   c)   assessing changing moods and opinions, primarily through interviews;
   d)   consequently making decisions about what works, and what does not.

4. Making changes as a result of the trial run means:
   a)   revising the schedule and advertisements accordingly;
   b)   continuing with advertising activities on a step-by-step basis;
   c)   being aware of ever-changing, internal and external factors;
   d)   pursuing a hands-on approach at all times, and never being afraid to make amendments, even to long-held beliefs.

Conclusion: the press advertiser's checklist

YOUR PRESS ADVERTISING CAMPAIGN hopefully will be a winner and certainly deserves to be if you tackle it in the correct, step-by-step manner. Nevertheless, if your future activities are to be equally successful, you need to continually review your knowledge of newspapers, magazines and miscellaneous publications as well as your approach to getting ready for, commencing and operating an advertising campaign in this medium. Only by looking backwards and constantly learning from the past can you look ahead and continue to succeed time and again.

Types of publication

❑ Are you totally familiar with the characteristics of and the similarities and dissimilarities between national daily and Sunday newspapers as well as regional dailies, Sundays, paid-for and free (bi-)weeklies?

❑ Do you know about the pros and cons of advertising in papers?

❑ Are you wholly aware of consumer and business magazines, especially their key, comparable and contrasting features?

❑ Do you recognize their benefits and drawbacks so far as advertisers are concerned?

❑ Have you taken full account of miscellaneous publications such as directories, brochures, in-house journals, timetables, maps and guidebooks?

❑ Do you appreciate the advantages and disadvantages which they offer to you?

Who's who in the press

❑ Are you conscious of the different departments and employees within a publication along with their work and the ways in which they interact with each other?

❑ Have you found out about the trade organizations in the press industry and how they can help you with your campaign?

❏   Do you know of the advertising bodies that may be involved with press advertising and understand what they do?

Analysing yourself

❏   Are you completely conversant with your own business and its distinctive blend of strengths and weaknesses?

❏   Have you studied the types of goods and services which you sell and verified their main features and plus and minus points?

❏   Are your short-, medium- and long-term objectives absolutely clear to you?

❏   Have you compiled detailed notes about your firm, products, services and goals for hands-on use during your advertising campaign?

Knowing your market

❏   Do you know everything about your existing and potential customers, especially their characteristics and their perceptions of you and your goods?

❏   Have you taken stock of all your present and possible rivals, assessing them in the same areas and ways in which you examined your own concern?

❏   Are you up-to-date about the internal workings of and external influences upon the market in which you operate or plan to operate?

❏   Have you carried out as much research as you can into your customers, competitors and marketplace, recording information to subsequently assist you throughout your advertising activities?

Establishing a budget

❏   Are the various methods used to calculate a suitable advertising budget familiar to you?

❏   Have you reviewed the past, looked at the present and anticipated the future before setting the appropriation?

❏   Do you keep abreast of changing and developing circumstances, making amendments to your budget whenever necessary?

Bringing in experts

❏   Have you ascertained the roles and services on offer from a full service agency, à la carte agency and a media independent?

❏   Are you aware of how to select such a specialist to administer or support you with your activities?

❏   Have you weighed up the possibilities of commissioning other experts to work on your behalf, namely a market research agency, an illustrator, a photographer, a copywriter and a typesetter?

❏   Do you know how to set about making the right choice for you?

Planning your schedule

❏   Do you draw up a shortlist of useable titles by reading through *British Rate and Data* and listening to recommendations from valid sources?

❏   Are media packs, rate cards and copies of the most recent issues always obtained and scanned from cover to cover?

❏   Do you compare and contrast each publication's audience with your own, retaining only those titles with similar profiles and extensive, in-depth penetration into your customer base?

❏   Have you thought about the timing, frequency and duration of your advertising activities, discarding the publications which do not allow you to promote yourself when you want to?

❏   Have you decided which sizes and positions are best for your advertisements and calculated the value-for-money costs of advertising in various titles?

❏   Do you constantly draft and redraft your schedule until it matches your allocated budget?

Creating your advertisements

❏   Are you conscious of the main features, pros and cons of display, semi-display and classified advertisements?

❏   Have you familiarized yourself with the multitude of approaches which can be adopted towards advertising, and settled upon one which seems suitable in your given situation?

❏   Have you thought about the layout of your advertisements?

❏   Have you considered the text of your advertisements?

❏   Do your advertisements remain within the law, being legal, decent, honest and truthful?

❏   Are they prepared with a sense of responsibility to your customers and competitors?

Buying advertising space

❏   Have you mastered the rate card, being able to translate all of its jargon?

❏   Are the terms and conditions of advertising in the press known to you?

❏   Are you capable of handling representatives properly, negotiating the best possible deals with them?

❏   Do you know how to work with the various titles to achieve success?

Conducting your activities

❏   Is a trial run always carried out to test your schedule and advertisements?

❏   Do you monitor responses to your advertising activities on an ongoing basis, using appropriate measurement techniques?

❏   Are changes made to your schedule and advertisements as and when necessary, even if it means admitting that firmly held beliefs are incorrect?

Appendix A: Media pack

INTRODUCTION

Welcome to the East Anglian Daily Times Company's Media Pack.
It has been prepared to help you understand the values of the
premier advertising media in the region.

As a company we realise fully that we are in business to help you grow your
businesses. To that end all our products and services are designed to help you
capitalise on the development of the region. The ranges of advertising vehicles and
services we provide ensure the maximum coverage of target markets within our
trading area.

The following information contains details gathered from a comprehensive study of
the media habits and readership patterns in our trading area. This was conducted
by BJM Research and Marketing Consultancy Limited in the spring of 1993.
Conforming fully to market research industry standards generally and the
specification of the Joint Industry Committee for Regional Press Research (JICREG)
in particular, the sample was based on interviews among over 1,000 adults in the
key circulation or distribution areas of the titles. As JICREG calculations of total
readership for each newspaper are based on the whole circulation or distribution
area, they include all readers outside the researched areas.

Much more information than is contained here is available to help maximise
the effectiveness of your media or market planning
- just ask your representative for full details.

With our range of newspapers, the audiences they deliver, the editorial
environments they provide and the creative opportunities they offer, you can be
assured we deliver the most flexible and cost-effective use of your promotional
budgets.

EAST ANGLIAN DAILY TIMES COMPANY LIMITED

THE EAST ANGLIAN DAILY TIMES COMPANY

Our company trades in Suffolk and North Essex, an area wholly within East Anglia. This area's economy has grown rapidly in the recent past yet it has retained the rural character which is one of its main attractions.

The prosperity of the potential marketplace is evidenced by the fact that East Anglia as a whole has now the highest Gross Domestic Product (GDP) per head outside of the South East and, despite the early 1990's recession, has the lowest rate of unemployment in the country.

Furthermore the area is forecast to resume its growth in GDP, consumer expenditure, industrial production, employment and population from the end of 1993 and to overtake the UK averages by 1995. As a consequence, this area was found to be the "Best of British" in terms of a Quality of Life survey carried out by The Economist in June 1993.

Publications and services offered to consumers in the area are -

The East Anglian Daily Times which has served the area every morning for nearly 120 years. It provides undisputedly the best coverage of its circulation area with its unique source of international, national, regional and local news and sport. The circulation area stretches through Suffolk from south Norfolk to south Essex and the three daily editions (East, West, Essex) ensure that the total of 151,618* adults who read the title in an average day receive their local national daily.

The Evening Star which is the evening paper for Ipswich and the surrounding area, is proud to cover its community. Published since 1885, it today has a direct freshness for campaigns, local as well as national and international news and sport delivered in a vigorous style to encourage interaction with its readers.

The total of 85,622 adults* who read the Evening Star in an average day are responsive and interested in their community - as evidenced by the high levels of entries to competitions, coupon redemptions on offers, readers' letters received and of course in the very high levels of response to advertising.

The Suffolk Mercury Series of free weekly newspapers which offer advertisers coverage of the whole county or, by buying combinations of the editions within the East or West Suffolk Mercury, specific coverage of distinct parts of Suffolk.
In an average week some 263,442 adults read a copy of the Suffolk Mercury.

Anglian Direct, the service for inserting pre-printed material into any edition of an East Anglian Daily Times Company daily or weekly publication and our **Business Magazines** division completes the range of coverage opportunities available to our advertisers.

Notes: HMSO Regional Trends 1993
     Financial Times 13.8.93
     *Joint Industry Committee for Regional Press Research, 1994

EAST ANGLIAN DAILY TIMES

ABC January - June 1994 49,494

The East Anglian Daily Times gives unrivalled media coverage of an area which spans the whole of Suffolk and North Essex in three daily editions. It caters for all sections of the region's population and is recognised as an important source of advertising information by its readers.

Independent market research has shown that:

* in an average day the East Anglian Daily Times is read by more than 137,000 adults - a higher readership figure than any other daily paper in the area;

* each copy of the East Anglian Daily Times is seen by at least 3 adults ensuring high coverage each day;

* more than half of the readers of the East Anglian Daily Times (54%) do not read any national newspaper - showing the influence of the title;

* on average readers spend 29 minutes reading their copy of the East Anglian Daily Times;

* the East Anglian Daily Times has a broad-based appeal and the readership profile is in line with that of the population as a whole;

* readership by day is balanced and the daily content ensures high interest throughout the week -
                    Monday: Sports coverage in depth
                    Tuesday: Job Centre ads, Regional News Round-Ups
                    Wednesday: Essex/Anglian Business Scene
                    Thursday: Recruitment, Property
                    Friday: Motors
                    Saturday: 48 Hours;

* 210,000 adults read at least one issue of the East Anglian Daily Times in an average week. An advertisement in 6 issues has the opportunity to be seen by 53% more adults than a single insertion - an extra 73,000 adults;

* the East Anglian Daily Times is the premier advertising medium in its area - more adults turn to it first for details about major purchases, property, jobs, local entertainment and second-hand items than to any other newspaper.

Notes: Research conducted by BJM Ltd., April 1993
        5%+ household penetration sample area (Base 1,017 adults)
        Readership = average issue readership, those reading for
        2 or more minutes in the issue period, ie yesterday.

EAST ANGLIAN
DAILY TIMES

ABC January - June 1994 49,494

EAST ANGLIAN
DAILY TIMES

ABC	Average Daily Sales JAN-JUNE 1994 — 49,494

The East Anglian Daily Times offers advertisers the most effective vehicle for covering Suffolk and North Essex.

RATES
ROP (PER S.C.C.) £6.40
PAGE 3 ....25% Surcharge
Other Premium Positions ......15% Surcharge
Front Page Solus £450.00
Title Corners ......Front £84.00, Back £47.00
Full Page......................................£1612.80
Half Page....................................£806..40

COLOUR CHARGES
Single Spot ....20% Extra
Multi Spot ....30% Extra
Full Process ....40% Extra

All rates subject to VAT

CLASSIFIED MARKET ADVERTISEMENT RATES

ABC	Average Daily Sales JAN-JUNE 1994 — 79,630

Classified Advertisements are published in the East Anglian Daily Times and the Evening Star.

RATES   (PER S.C.C.)
Display
Situations Vacant £14.25
Motors £8.50
Property £8.25
Others £10.40
Public Notices/Tenders £11.00
Auctions £8.25
(Box Numbers ....£10.00)

LINAGE   (PER LINE)
Private/Trade £2.21
Situations Vacant £2.70
(Box Numbers Charged at 4 Lines)
All rates are subject to VAT

SUPPLEMENTARY INFORMATION

TECHNICAL DATA

Column length 360 mm; screen 35 per cm.
7 columns per page display,
8 columns per page classified.
Production —
Photosetting, artwork, bromides or original photographs required.
Blocks or mats not acceptable.
Printed web offset. Studio design and artwork service available at no extra charge.

COLUMN WIDTHS (mm)

Columns	Display (7 cols. per page)	Classified (8 cols. per page)
1	36	31
2	75	65
3	115	100
4	154	134
5	194	168
6	233	203
7	273	237
8	-	272

DEADLINES (CLEAR WORKING DAYS)

Colour
Full Colour......10 Days
Multi Spot........5 Days
Spot Colour......2 Days

ORDER & COPY (MONO)

East Anglian Daily Times } 48 hours prior
Evening Star   } to publication.

PROOFS

3 full days must be given for any proof requests.
See Item 13 Terms & Conditions

EAST ANGLIAN DAILY TIMES COMPANY
Head Office: Press House, 30 Lower Brook Street, Ipswich IP4 1AN
Telephone: (01473) 230023 Telex: 98172 Fax: (01473) 232529 Ad Doc: Dx 3261 Ipswich

Branch Offices -
BURY ST. EDMUNDS Lloyds Bank Chambers, Buttermarket. Tel: (01284) 702588 Fax: 702970
FELIXSTOWE 120 Hamilton Road. Tel: (01394) 284109 Fax: 284994
STOWMARKET 1 Market Place. Tel: (01449) 674428 Fax: 774301
SUDBURY 1 King Street. Tel: (01787) 72242 Fax: 79157
HALESWORTH 16 Thoroughfare. Tel: (01986) 872202 Fax: 875338
LEISTON 72 High Street. Tel: (01728) 830472 Fax: 832187
COLCHESTER Dugard House, Moss Road, Stanway. Tel: (01206) 769212 Fax: 577857
WOODBRIDGE Barton House, 84 The Thoroughfare. Tel: (01394) 385353 Fax: 387025

AMRA
London Office: Park Place, 12 Lawn Lane, Vauxhall, London SW8 1UD
Tel: 0171 820 1000. Fax: 0171 820 0304/5
Ad Doc: Dx 2327 Victoria.
Manchester Office: Byrom House, Quay Street, Manchester M3 3HG
Tel: 0161 834 2050. Fax: 0161 835 2781
Ad Doc: Dx 18157 Manchester 3

Rates Effective from 3rd October 1994

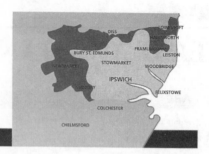

EVENING STAR

ABC January - June 1994 30,136

The Evening Star has the highest readership penetration of any daily paper in its area and is followed in penetration by its sister paper the East Anglian Daily Times. Readership of the national dailies in the area is depressed by the presence of such strong evening and morning titles.

Independent market research has shown that:

* in an average day the Evening Star reaches 71,000 adults - 40% of the total population aged over 15 in the survey area. When total readership is included, this figure rises to 86,000 adults who read the Evening Star on an average day;

* each copy of the Evening Star is read by 2.8 readers - ensuring high daily coverage;

* a very high proportion of readers (6 in 10) have their Evening Star delivered to their homes, showing the commitment of readers to the title;

* the Evening Star has a particular appeal for those aged 45-64, the C2DE social grades and women. Unlike many regional / local dailies it has a better penetration of non-working than working people;

* readership by day is constant and the daily content ensures high interest throughout the week -
     Monday: Weekend Sports Round-Up
     Tuesday: Job Centre ads
     Wednesday: Commercial Property
     Thursday: Recruitment, Property
     Friday: Motors
     Saturday: Weekender;

* in an average week 94,000 adults read at least one issue of the Evening Star. This means that the potential audience of a series of six consecutive insertions rather than one stand-alone advertisement is increased by one third;

* on average each reader spends 29 minutes reading the Evening Star - evidence of a "well-read" paper;

* the Evening Star is a major source of advertising information with more adults turning to it first for details of jobs, property, major purchases, second-hand items and local entertainment than to any other newspaper in its area.

Notes: Research conducted by BJM Ltd., April 1993
          10%+ household penetration sample area (Base 503 adults)
          Readership = average issue readership, those reading for
          2 or more minutes in the issue period, ie yesterday.

Evening Star

ABC January - June 1994 30,136

Evening Star

| ABC | Average Daily Sales
JAN-JUNE 1994 — 30,136 |

First with local news, sport and entertainment, the Evening Star covers Ipswich and the surrounding area.

RATES
ROP (PER S.C.C.)..............................£5.50
PAGE 3...............................25% Surcharge
Other Premium Positions .....15% Surcharge
Front Page Solus...........................£315.00
Title Corners......Front £47.00, Back £19.00
Full Page.....................................£1386.00
Half Page......................................£693.00

COLOUR CHARGES
Single Spot ....20% Extra
Multi Spot ....30% Extra
Full Process ....40% Extra

All rates subject to VAT

CLASSIFIED MARKET ADVERTISEMENT RATES

| ABC | Average Daily Sales
JAN-JUNE 1994 — 79,630 |

Classified Advertisements are published in the East Anglian Daily Times and the Evening Star.

RATES   (PER S.C.C.)
Display
Situations Vacant £14.25
Motors £8.50
Property £8.25
Others £10.40
Public Notices/Tenders £11.00
Auctions £8.25
(Box Numbers ....£10.00)

LINAGE   (PER LINE)
Private/Trade £2.21
Situations Vacant £2.70
(Box Numbers Charged at 4 Lines)
All rates are subject to VAT

SUPPLEMENTARY INFORMATION

TECHNICAL DATA

Column length 360 mm; screen 35 per cm.
7 columns per page display,
8 columns per page classified.
Production —
Photosetting, artwork, bromides or
original photographs required.
Blocks or mats not acceptable.
Printed web offset. Studio design
and artwork service available
at no extra charge.

COLUMN WIDTHS (mm)

| Columns | Display
(7 cols. per page) | Classified
(8 cols. per page) |
|---------|---------|-----------|
| 1 | 36 | 31 |
| 2 | 75 | 65 |
| 3 | 115 | 100 |
| 4 | 154 | 134 |
| 5 | 194 | 168 |
| 6 | 233 | 203 |
| 7 | 273 | 237 |
| 8 | - | 272 |

DEADLINES (CLEAR WORKING DAYS)

Colour
Full Colour......10 Days
Multi Spot........5 Days
Spot Colour...... 2 Days

ORDER & COPY (MONO)

East Anglian Daily Times　}　48 hours prior
Evening Star　　　　　　　　to publication.

PROOFS

3 full days must be given
for any proof requests.
See Item 13 Terms & Conditions

EAST ANGLIAN DAILY TIMES COMPANY
Head Office: Press House, 30 Lower Brook Street, Ipswich IP4 1AN
Telephone: (01473) 230023 Telex: 98172 Fax: (01473) 232529 Ad Doc: Dx 3261 Ipswich

Branch Offices -
BURY ST. EDMUNDS Lloyds Bank Chambers, Buttermarket. Tel: (01284) 702588 Fax: 702970
FELIXSTOWE 120 Hamilton Road. Tel:(01394) 284109 Fax: 284994
STOWMARKET 1 Market Place. Tel: (01449) 674428 Fax: 774301
SUDBURY 1 King Street. Tel: (01787) 72242 Fax: 79157
HALESWORTH 16 Thoroughfare. Tel: (01986) 872202 Fax: 875338
LEISTON 72 High Street. Tel: (01728) 830472 Fax: 832187
COLCHESTER Dugard House, Moss Road, Stanway. Tel: (01206) 769212 Fax: 577857
WOODBRIDGE Barton House, 84 The Thoroughfare. Tel: (01394) 385353 Fax: 387025

AMRA
London Office: Park Place, 12 Lawn Lane,
Vauxhall, London SW8 1UD
Tel: 0171 820 1000. Fax: 0171 820 0304/5
Ad Doc: Dx 2327 Victoria.
Manchester Office: Byrom House,
Quay Street, Manchester M3 3HG
Tel: 0161 834 2050. Fax: 0161 835 2781
Ad Doc: Dx 18157 Manchester 3

Rates Effective from 3rd October 1994

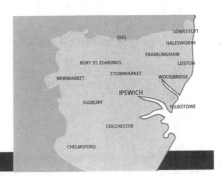

THE CLASSIFIED SECTION

EAST ANGLIAN DAILY TIMES AND EVENING STAR

Carried within both daily titles the Classified Section of the East Anglian Daily Times and Evening Star provides a major attraction and focal point to both newspapers.
Duplicate readership of both papers is very small (3% of all adults) as very few adults read both in an average day. Together the East Anglian Daily Times and Evening Star reach more than 205,000 adults in an average day.

Categories covered daily include -

> Auctions
> Business and Finance, Office Equipment
> Agricultural, Farming, Plant & Machinery, Poultry & Livestock
> Recruitment, General Vacancies, Hotel & Catering, Part-time, Training Courses
> Property, Accommodation to Let, Commercial, Building Land, Overseas
> Motors, New & Used, Accessories, Spares, Service, Vehicle Hire
> Leisure, Hobbies, Boating & Yachting, Holidays, Caravans, Horse & Rider
> General and Home Services, Personal, Dental, Catering, Builders, Landscape Gardening
> Miscellaneous Sales, Pets, Musical, Articles for Sale/Wanted
> Public and Legal Notices, Tenders & Contracts

Each week there are special supplements dedicated to Property (Thursday); Motors (Friday); as well as comprehensive coverage of all Recruitment advertisements on Thursdays.

The Classified advertising sections in both the East Anglian Daily Times and Evening Star reach significant proportions of the population - more than 299,000 adults in an average year .

* 126,000 readers of the East Anglian Daily Times read the
  Classified Section at least once a week, 187,000 read it at all;

* 57,000 readers of the Evening Star read the Classified Section
  at least once a week, 90,000 read it at all;

* 60,000 adults placed an advertisement in the East Anglian
  Daily Times in the last year - 96,000 responded;

* 37,000 adults placed an advertisement in the Evening Star
  in the last year - 60,000 responded.

Notes: Research conducted by BJM Ltd., April 1993
        5%+ household penetration area (Base 1,017 adults)
        Readership = average issue readership, those reading for
        2 or more minutes in the issue period, ie yesterday.

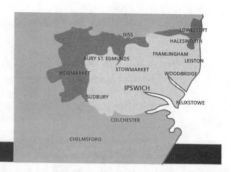

SUFFOLK MERCURY SERIES

VFD January - June 1994:
Whole series - 157,122
East - 110,284 (Ipswich 86,041; Stowmarket 12,219; North 12,024)
West - 46,838 (Bury St. Edmunds 27,219; Sudbury 19,619)

Covering the major areas of Suffolk, the Suffolk Mercury series has high levels of penetration and readership each week. Specific editions for individual areas ensure that Suffolk Mercury editorial is relevant to readers.

Independent market research has shown that:

* 76% of adults aged 15 or over read the Mercury in an average week - some 265,000 adults;

* 182,000 adults read the East Suffolk edition (75% penetration) and 84,000 adults read the West Suffolk edition (78% penetration);

* the Mercury overall has 1.7 readers per copy - a good figure for a free newspaper (East Suffolk Mercury 1.6, the West Suffolk Mercury 1.8 readers per copy);

* a high proportion of adults, 88% receive the Mercury every or most weeks, proof of the effective distribution system;

* the sex profile of readers exactly matches the profile of the area as a whole and generally readers are likely to be slightly older and less upmarket than the total population in the area;

* on average readers spend 16 minutes reading the Mercury - 15 minutes the East Suffolk Mercury and 17 minutes the West Suffolk Mercury.

Notes: Research conducted by BJM Ltd., April 1993
   10%+ household distribution sample area (Base 810 adults)
   Readership = average issue readership, those reading for 2 or more minutes in the issue period, ie last 7 days.

Mercury

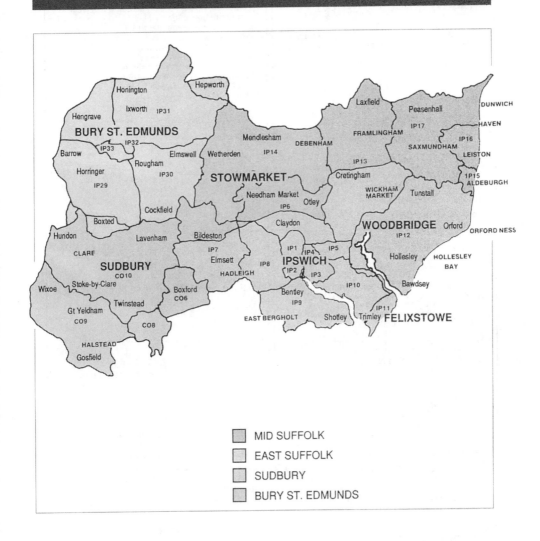

- MID SUFFOLK
- EAST SUFFOLK
- SUDBURY
- BURY ST. EDMUNDS

(**VFD**) January - June 1994 157,122

Mercury

 East Suffolk Mercury 110,284
West Suffolk Mercury 46,838
Jan–Jun 1994

The Mercury series are the leading free weekly newspapers. They are divided into East and West Suffolk and offer advertisers the most comprehensive coverage of the area.

RATE (P.S.C.C.)	EAST		WEST	
ROP	£6.60		£3.80	
Guaranteed Position	25% Surcharge		25% Surcharge	
	Display	Linage	Display	Linage
Situation Vacant	£16.20		£6.75	
Motors	£5.66	—	£4.12	—
Property	£5.66	—	£4.12	—
Others	£6.20	—	£3.95	—
Public Notices	£11.55	—	£4.65	—
Box Numbers	£10.00 (4 Lines)		£10.00 (4 Lines)	

Separate Edition Rates on request.

All rates subject to VAT.

The separate editorial editions ensure that each area has its own local news and stories relevant to its distribution area. Thus advertisers have a variety of unique vehicles by which to convey a sales message.

The East Suffolk Mercury, operating from the Ipswich Head Office, has two advertising editions, East Suffolk and Mid Suffolk (including North Suffolk and Stowmarket). Tel. 01473 230023.

The West Suffolk Mercury, situated in Bury St. Edmunds itself, has two editions, (Bury and Sudbury).
Tel. Sudbury 01787 72242
Tel. Bury St. Edmunds 01284 702588

SUPPLEMENTARY INFORMATION

TECHNICAL DATA

Column length 360 mm; screen 35 per cm.
7 columns per page display,
8 columns per page classified.
Production —
Photosetting, artwork, bromides or original photographs required.
Blocks or mats not acceptable.
Printed web offset. Studio design and artwork service available at no extra charge.

COLUMN WIDTHS (mm)

Columns	Display (7 cols. per page)	Classified (8 cols. per page)
1	36	31
2	75	65
3	115	100
4	154	134
5	194	168
6	233	203
7	273	237
8	-	272

DEADLINES (CLEAR WORKING DAYS)

Colour
Full Colour......10 Days
Multi Spot........5 Days
Spot Colour......2 Days

ORDER & COPY (MONO)

East Suffolk Mercury
West Suffolk Mercury
} Orders Friday prior to publication. Copy Monday 12 noon prior to publication.

PROOFS

3 full days must be given for any proof requests.
See Item 13 Terms & Conditions

EAST ANGLIAN DAILY TIMES COMPANY

Head Office: Press House, 30 Lower Brook Street, Ipswich IP4 1AN
Telephone: (01473) 230023 Telex: 98172 Fax: (01473) 232529 Ad Doc: Dx 3261 Ipswich

Branch Offices -
BURY ST. EDMUNDS Lloyds Bank Chambers, Buttermarket. Tel: (01284) 702588 Fax: 702970
FELIXSTOWE 120 Hamilton Road. Tel: (01394) 284109 Fax: 284994
STOWMARKET 1 Market Place. Tel: (01449) 674428 Fax:774301
SUDBURY 1 King Street. Tel: (01787) 72242 Fax: 79157
HALESWORTH 16 Thoroughfare. Tel: (01986) 872202 Fax: 875338
LEISTON 72 High Street. Tel: (01728) 830472 Fax: 832187
COLCHESTER Dugard House, Moss Road, Stanway. Tel: (01206) 769212 Fax: 577857
WOODBRIDGE Barton House, 84 The Thoroughfare. Tel: (01394) 385353 Fax: 387025

AMRA
London Office: Park Place, 12 Lawn Lane,
Vauxhall, London SW8 1UD
Tel: 0171 820 1000. Fax: 0171 820 0304/5
Ad Doc: Dx 2327 Victoria.
Manchester Office: Byrom House,
Quay Street, Manchester M3 3HG
Tel: 0161 834 2050. Fax: 0161 835 2781
Ad Doc: Dx 18157 Manchester 3

Rates Effective from 3rd October 1994

SERVICES FOR ADVERTISERS

The following services have been developed to help our advertisers maximise their investments in advertising. This list does not cover every need or indeed every service we can provide. If you would like more information about how we can enhance your marketing effort please talk to your representative.

Campaign Planning: our advertising staff are trained to help increase the effectiveness of clients' campaigns and are able to assist in planning the most effective use of local media to achieve both marketing and media objectives.

Partnership Marketing: involves both retailers and manufacturers in the funding of advertisements to further the advertising and promotion of goods for sale. Supported by the Newspaper Society the EADT Company is able to identify suppliers who will provide financial or creative support for local advertising.
Contact : 01473 282340

Anglian Direct: caters for clients wishing to use Leaflets, Brochures or Coupons to promote their goods or services and offers precise targeting or blanket coverage throughout Suffolk and North Essex.

Leaflets or other suitable material can be inserted directly into any of the newspapers for maximum impact. Alternatively leaflets can be delivered in the traditional manner for precisely defined areas.
Contact : 01473 282215

Creative Services: our Design studio can give help on the design, layout and content of advertisements. Creative ideas can be carried through to full artwork.

Box Numbers: we offer a private and confidential advertisement reply service where all responses can be forwarded to advertisers or collected in person from our Ipswich office.

Research and Marketing Data: our consumer research data and information covering details about markets, the area, its inhabitants and their media habits are available to clients to help in the planning, accomplishment and evaluation of advertising campaigns.

The information ranges from our own commissioned research to market reports and government information - including the 1991 census - and also includes MOSAIC - a geo-demographic classification system.

CONDITIONS OF ACCEPTANCE FOR ADVERTISEMENTS

1 We reserve the right to refuse to insert any advertisement even though accepted and paid for and to make any alterations we deem necessary to maintain our standards.

2 The publisher shall not be liable for any loss or damage occasioned by any total or partial failure (however caused) of publication or distribution of any newspaper or edition in which any advertisement is scheduled to appear.

3 In the event of any error, misprint or omission in the printing of any advertisement or part of an advertisement the publisher will either re-insert the advertisement or relevant part of the advertisement as the case may be or make a reasonable refund or adjustment to the cost. No re-insertion, refund or adjustment will be made where the error, misprint or omission does not materially detract from the advertisement. In no circumstances shall the total liability of the publisher for any error, misprint or omission exceed the amount of a full refund of any price paid to the publisher for the particular advertisement in connection with which liability arose or the cost of a further or corrective advertisement of a type and standard reasonably comparable to that in connection with which liability arose.

4 Advertisements which do not conform to the Trade Descriptions Act, 1968, the Sex Discriminations Act, 1975, the Business Advertisements (Disclosure) Order, 1977 and other relevant legislation will be refused.

5 We do not accept liability for any loss or damage incurred by advertisers allegedly arising in respect of loss, damage or non-receipt of box number replies, save where such loss or damage has arisen directly as a result of our negligence.

6 Advertisers cancelling advertisements will be given a Stop Number which must be quoted in subsequent inquiries. Cancellation of "till discontinued" bookings must be confirmed by a letter addressed to the General Advertisement Manager.

7 Mistakes that arise in the course of publication must be notified to us within one week of insertion. After that time claims for credit cannot be considered.

8 Participation in advertisement features and supplements does not imply any editorial mention.

9 Advertisers placing pre-paid classified advertisements are responsible for checking that the published advertisement matches the charge made. Requests for adjustments, accompanied by the official receipt, should be made to branch or head offices.

10 We do not hold ourselves responsible for the loss of artwork or photographs supplied.

11 Advertisements ordered for the Classified Section will appear in both the East Anglian Daily Times and the Evening Star except on Public Holidays when they could appear in one title only and normal rates will apply.

12 Cancellations: No cancellations to bookings will be accepted for special positions or features within 10 clear working days of publication and for all other advertisements 2 clear working days prior to publication.

13 Proofs: No alterations to proofs will be made other than for spelling, grammar or factual information that differs from the copy supplied.

14 The quality of our reproductions is dependent upon the quality of the original material, photographs, artwork or bromides which are supplied. Should there be any doubt regarding the suitability for reproduction of any of these prior to publication advice can be obtained from our staff.

15 We reserve the right to open or withhold any box number correspondence should it be deemed necessary in the public interest.

SPECIAL NOTICE

All gross advertising rates (except classified lineage and semi-display) are subject to a 0.1% Advertising Standards Board of Finance surcharge payable by advertisers, to help finance the self-regulatory control system administered by the Advertising Standards Authority.

ADVERTISING RATES (effective 8.10.95)

Daily titles: *East Anglian Times and Evening Star*

Classified Market	Display	Linage
Recruitment	£15.50 per scc	£3 per line
Motors	£8.80 per scc	£2.30 per line
Property	£8.55 per scc	£2.30 per line
Others	£10.75 per scc	£2.30 per line
ROP		
(EA)	£6.65 per scc	
(ES)	£5.70 per scc	
Legal Notices	£11.40 per scc	

Weekly titles:	*East Suffolk Mercury*	*West Suffolk Mercury*
	Display	**Display**
Recruitment	£17.50	£7.10
Motors	£5.90	£4.30
Property	£5.90	£4.30
Others	£6.45	£4.15
ROP	£6.85	£3.95

All charges exclude VAT; all display charges per scc; min. sizes 3cms or 3 lines.

SERVICES AVAILABLE INCLUDE:
Campaign planning;
Partnership marketing;
Anglian Direct – leaflet distribution;
Creative services;
Research and marketing

Appendix B: Rate cards

IN APPENDIX A, you will have read about three local newspapers and typically you will advertise in publications such as these. Here are rate cards for national newspapers and magazines. Even though you may not advertise in them this time around, it is useful to study them to increase your knowledge and understanding, and for future reference.

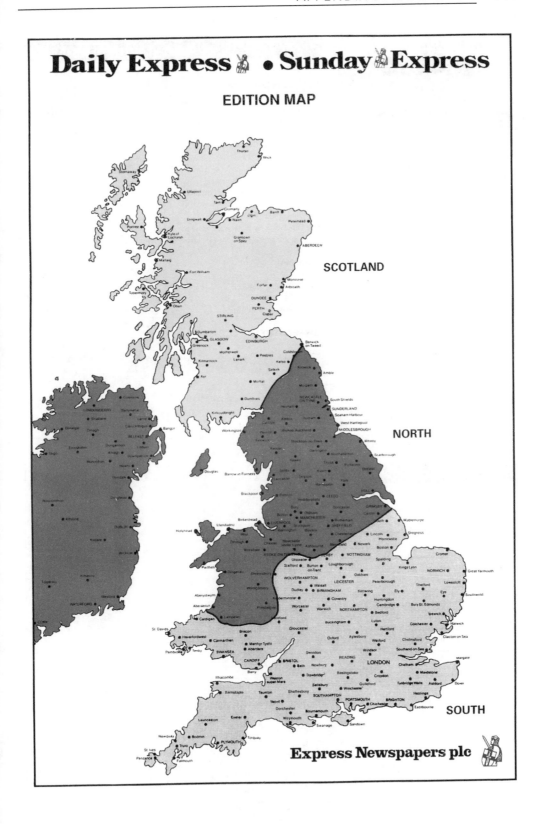

DISPLAY MONO (Minimum 3scc's)	**scc**
Firm Day	£44.00
Run of Week	£38.50
(Page Size - 35cm x 7 columns = 245cm)	

DISPLAY OTR COLOUR	
Page	£15,092

FEATURES (Minimum 3scc's)	**scc**
Holidays & Travel, Gardening, Postal Bargains	£38.50

SPECIAL POSITIONS

Back Page Solus (up to 15cm x 2 columns)	£1,320

(Other special positions and A/B and North/South copy splits subject to 10% surcharge)

REGIONAL	**scc**
Scotland	£10.00
North (excluding Scotland)	£27.50
South	£22.00
London and the South East	£15.00

ADVERTISEMENT FEATURES	**page**
Mono	£13,475
OTR Colour	£18,865
Sponsorship Rates	On application

NAMES & EXTENSIONS

(All numbers act as direct lines if prefixed by 0171-922 or as extensions off the main switchboard)

Advertisement Controller
Howard Warren 2720
Advertisement Manager
Philip Snowdon 2770
Group Heads
Harry Torrance 2766
Janey Pilkington 2755
Travel
Keith Cartwright 2814
Financial
Paul Reynolds 2733
Mail Order
Terry O'Connor 2773
Advertisement Features
Ian Hockridge 2747
Heather Murphy 2792
Inserts
Mike Winston 2797
Research
Stuart Corke 2862

EXPRESS GROUP

Advertisement Director
Christine Costello 2727
Deputy Advertisement Director
Julie France 2754
Research & Sales Support Director
Iain McLellan 2868
Client Sales Controller
Patrick Chaundy 2803
Contracts Controller
Mike Baker 2704
Financial Advertisement Manager
Peter Thompson 2732
Travel Advertisement Manager
Glynis Jeffery 2779
Regional Advertisement Manager
Chris Skinner 2788

Express Newspapers plc
Ludgate House
245 Blackfriars Road
London SE1 9UX
Tel: 0171-928 8000
Fax: 0171-620 1646

**Ratecard effective from
October 1995**

MAKE-UP

(All numbers act as direct lines if prefixed by 0171-922 or as extensions off the main switchboard)

**Group Advertisement
Make-up Manager**
Steve Sherer   2832
Colour Production Manager
Karen Miller   7255

DAILY STAR MECHANICAL DATA

1 column width	37mm	5 column width	197mm
2 column width	77mm	6 column width	237mm
3 column width	117mm	7 column width	275mm
4 column width	157mm		

Total Page Area	345mm x 275mm

COLOUR SPECIFICATION

Material supplied for colour advertisement reproduction in the Daily Star must be either artwork and transparencies, CMYK separated data or RGB data and artwork (or disk).

All colour advertisement material should be sent to Digital Partnership Limited at the Express Newspapers address.

All colour advertisement material must be supplied at least 72 hours prior to publication.

For more information please contact Digital Partnership Limited on 0171-922 7374 or Express Newspapers Colour Production Manager on 0171-922 7255.

Daily Express

Daily Express

NAMES & EXTENSIONS

(All numbers act as direct lines if
prefixed by 0171-922 or as
extensions off the main switchboard)

Advertisement Controller
Georgina Crace   2782
**Daily Express
Advertisement Manager**
Charles McCrostie   2784
**This Week
Advertisement Manager**
Chris Morris   2706
Group Heads
Jo Fullbrook   2916
Neil McQuillan   2830
Fiona Nobles   2929
Travel
Keith Cartwright   2814
Financial
Simon Haque   2735
Mail Order
Terry O'Connor   2773
Advertisement Features
Ian Hockridge   2747
Heather Murphy   2792
Inserts
Mike Winston   2797
Research
Stuart Corke   2862

EXPRESS GROUP

Advertisement Director
Christine Costello   2727
Deputy Advertisement Director
Julie France   2754
Research & Sales Support Director
Iain McLellan   2868
Client Sales Controller
Patrick Chaundy   2803
Contracts Controller
Mike Baker   2704
Financial Advertisement Manager
Peter Thompson   2732
Travel Advertisement Manager
Glynis Jeffery   2779
Regional Advertisement Manager
Chris Skinner   2788

DAILY EXPRESS ADVERTISEMENT RATES

DISPLAY MONO (Minimum 3scc's)   **scc**
Firm Day   **£97.00**
Run of Week   **£85.00**
(Page Size - 35cm x 7 columns = 245cm)

DISPLAY OTR COLOUR
Page   **£31,500**

FEATURES (Minimum 5scc's)   **scc**
Holidays & Travel, Gardening, Postal Bargains   **£85.00**
Express Money   **£97.00**

SPECIAL POSITIONS
Back Page Solus (20cm x 2 columns)   **£4,250**
Express Money Front Page Earpiece (4cm x 1 column) **£500**
(Other special positions and A/B and North/South copy splits subject to 10% surcharge)

REGIONAL   **scc**
Scotland   **£19.00**
North (excluding Scotland)   **£36.50**
South   **£60.50**
London and the South East   **£55.00**

ADVERTISEMENT FEATURES   **page**
Mono   **£29,706**
OTR Colour   **£39,375**
Sponsorship Rates   On application

THIS WEEK ADVERTISEMENT RATES

DISPLAY COLOUR   **page**
Run of Paper   **£27,500**
Outside Back Cover   **£32,000**
Inside Front/Back Cover   **£30,000**

ADVERTISEMENT FEATURES
Page   **£34,375**
Sponsorship Rates   On application

INSERTS
(Loose or stitched available by ISBA region)
Under 100,000   **£30** (per 1,000)
Over 100,000   **£25** (per 1,000)
16 pages or above subject to 20% surcharge
Minimum volume 25,000
Special printing facilities ie fragrance and gummed cards on request

Daily Express

DAILY EXPRESS MECHANICAL DATA

I column width	37mm	5 column width	197mm
2 column width	77mm	6 column width	237mm
3 column width	117mm	7 column width	275mm
4 column width	157mm		

Total Page Area   345mm x 275mm

COLOUR SPECIFICATION

Material supplied for colour advertisement reproduction in the Daily Express
must be either artwork and transparencies, CMYK separated data or RGB
data and artwork (or disk).

All colour advertisement material should be sent to Digital Partnership
Limited at the Express Newspapers address.

All colour advertisement material must be supplied at least 72 hours prior to
publication.

For more information please contact Digital Partnership Limited on
0171-922 7374 or Express Newspapers Colour Production Manager on
0171-922 7255.

THIS WEEK MECHANICAL DATA

	Depth Width
Full page (Trimmed)	367 x 270mm
Double Page Spread (Trimmed)	367 x 540mm
Page (Untrimmed Bleed)	377 x 280mm
Double Page Spread (Untrimmed Bleed)	377 x 550mm
Page (Type Area)	335 x 245mm
Double Page Spread (Type Area)	335 x 511mm

COLOUR SPECIFICATION
Refer to Express Newspapers' Colour Specification Guidelines or contact
Karen Miller.
Inserts
Refer to Express Newspapers' Inserts Guidelines or contact Karen Miller.

Express Newspapers plc
Ludgate House
245 Blackfriars Road
London SE1 9UX
Tel: 0171-928 8000
Fax: 0171-620 1646

**Ratecard effective from
October 1995**

NAMES & EXTENSIONS

(All numbers act as direct lines if prefixed by 0171-922 or as extensions off the main switchboard)

Advertisement Controller
Simon Young   2721
Advertisement Manager
Shalene Perkins   2808
Group Heads
David Rossiter   2810
Gaby Fireman   2713
Travel
Keith Cartwright   2814
Financial
Mark Finney   2734
Mail Order
Terry O'Connor   2773
Advertisement Features
Ian Hockridge   2747
Heather Murphy   2792
Inserts
Mike Winston   2797
Research
Stuart Corke   2862

EXPRESS GROUP

Advertisement Director
Christine Costello   2727
Deputy Advertisement Director
Julie France   2754
Research & Sales Support Director
Iain McLellan   2868
Client Sales Controller
Patrick Chaundy   2803
Contracts Controller
Mike Baker   2704
Financial Advertisement Manager
Peter Thompson   2732
Travel Advertisement Manager
Glynis Jeffery   2779
Regional Advertisement Manager
Chris Skinner   2788

DISPLAY MONO (Minimum 3scc's)	scc
Firm Day	£116.00
2 Week Option	£105.00
(Page Size - 35cm x 7 columns = 245cm)	
(Large sizes, above 25cm high and/or 5 columns, and guaranteed positions subject to 10% surcharge)	
Half Page Horizontal	£16,916
Full Page Firm Day	£30,960
Full Page 2 Week Option	£29,864
DISPLAY OTR COLOUR	
Full Page Front Half	£40,725
Full Page Back Half	£38,623
SPECIAL POSITIONS	
First Right/Left Hand Page	£37,670
Second Right Hand Page	£35,713
Back Page Solus (15cm x 2 columns)	£7,700
(Other special positions subject to 10% surcharge)	
FINANCIAL	
Full Page Firm Day	£30,960
Full Page 2 Week Option	£29,864
REGIONAL	scc
Scotland	£11.00
North (excluding Scotland)	£37.00
South	£85.00
London and the South East	On application
North/South Copy Splits	£500
ADVERTISEMENT FEATURES	page
Mono	£32,156
OTR Colour	£50,906
Sponsorship Rates	On application

MAKE-UP

(All numbers act as direct lines if
prefixed by 0171-922 or as
extensions off the main switchboard)

Group Advertisement
Make-up Manager
Steve Sherer   2832
Colour Production Manager
Karen Miller   7255

SUNDAY EXPRESS MECHANICAL DATA

1 column width	37mm	5 column width	197mm
2 column width	77mm	6 column width	237mm
3 column width	117mm	7 column width	275mm
4 column width	157mm		

Total Page Area		345mm x 275mm

COLOUR SPECIFICATION

Material supplied for colour advertisement reproduction in the Sunday Express
must be either artwork and transparencies, CMYK separated data or RGB
data and artwork (or disk).

All colour advertisement material should be sent to Digital Partnership
Limited at the Express Newspapers address.

All colour advertisement material must be supplied at least 72 hours prior to
publication.

For more information please contact Digital Partnership Limited on
0171-922 7374 or Express Newspapers Colour Production Manager on
0171-922 7255.

Express Newspapers plc
Ludgate House
245 Blackfriars Road
London SE1 9UX
Tel: 0171-928 8000
Fax: 0171-620 1646

Ratecard effective from
October 1995

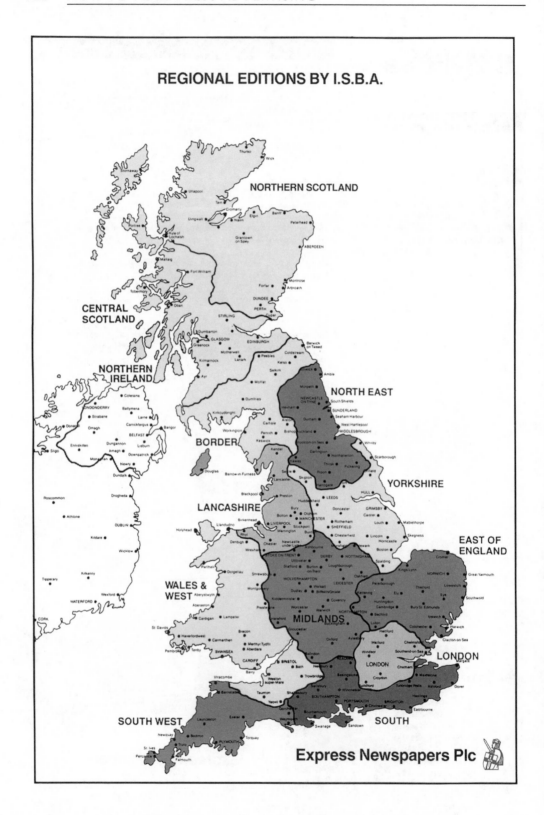

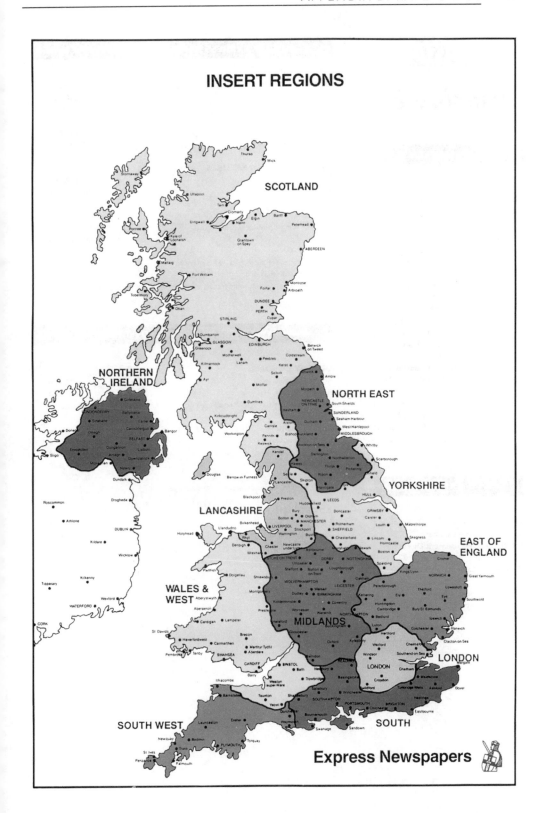

SUNDAY EXPRESS MAGAZINE

(All numbers act as direct lines if prefixed by 0171-922 or as extensions off the main switchboard)

Advertisement Controller
Simon Young 2721
Advertisement Manager
Andy Farthing 2724
Group Heads
Kieran Kelly 2726
Alan Totten 2758
Travel
Keith Cartwright 2814
Financial
Mark Finney 2734
Advertisement Features
Ian Hockridge 2747
Heather Murphy 2792
Inserts
Mike Winston 2797
Research
Stuart Corke 2862

EXPRESS GROUP

Advertisement Director
Christine Costello 2727
Deputy Advertisement Director
Julie France 2754
Research & Sales Support Director
Iain McLellan 2868
Client Sales Controller
Patrick Chaundy 2803
Contracts Controller
Mike Baker 2704
Financial Advertisement Manager
Peter Thompson 2732
Travel Advertisement Manager
Glynis Jeffery 2779
Regional Advertisement Manager
Liz Mathams 2798

SUNDAY EXPRESS CLASSIC ADVERTISEMENT RATES

DISPLAY COLOUR | page
Run of Magazine | £30,000

Special Positions
Outside Back Cover | £35,000
Inside Back/Front Cover | £32,500

ADVERTISEMENT FEATURES
Page | £37,500
Sponsorship Rates | On application

INSERTS
(Loose or stitched available by ISBA region)
Under 100,000 | £30 (per 1,000)
Over 100,000 | £25 (per 1,000)
16 pages or above subject to 20% surcharge
Minimum volume 25,000
Special printing facilities ie fragrance and gummed cards on request

SUNDAY EXPRESS MAGAZINE ADVERTISEMENT RATES

DISPLAY COLOUR
Run of Magazine, Page | £22,400
Run of Magazine, Half Page | £13,600
Quarter and Eighth Pages/Mono Pages | On application

Special Positions | page
Outside Back Cover | £36,050
Inside Back Cover | £30,000
Inside Front Cover | £34,600
First Spread | £58,100
(Other special positions subject to a 10% surcharge)

ADVERTISEMENT FEATURES
Page | £28,000
Sponsorship Rates | On application

INSERTS
As above

Classic

SUNDAY & EXPRESS
magazine

MAKE-UP

(All numbers act as direct lines if
prefixed by 0171-922 or as
extensions off the main switchboard)

**Group Advertisement
Make-up Manager**
Steve Sherer   2832
Colour Production Manager
Karen Miller   7255

SUNDAY EXPRESS CLASSIC MECHANICAL DATA

	Depth Width
Full Page (Type Area)	332 x 235mm
Full Page (Untrimmed Bleed)	373 x 276mm
Full Page (Trimmed Bleed)	367 x 270mm
Half Page Across (Type Area)	163 x 235mm
Half Page Across (Untrimmed Bleed)	186 x 276mm
Half Page Across (Trimmed Bleed)	180 x 270mm
Half Page Upright (Type Area)	332 x 114mm
Half Page Upright (Untrimmed Bleed)	373 x 137mm
Half Page Upright (Trimmed Bleed)	367 x 131mm
Half Page Spread (Type Area)	163 x 504mm
Half Page Spread (Untrimmed Bleed)	186 x 546mm
Half Page Spread (Trimmed Bleed)	180 x 540mm
Double Page Spread (Type Area)	332 x 504mm
Double Page Spread (Untrimmed Bleed)	373 x 546mm
Double Page Spread (Trimmed Bleed)	367 x 540mm

SUNDAY EXPRESS MAGAZINE MECHANICAL DATA

	Depth Width
Full page (Type Area)	259 x 200mm
Full Page (Untrimmed Bleed)	292 x 231mm
Full Page (Trimmed Bleed)	286 x 225mm
Double Page Spread (Gutter Bleed)	259 x 422mm
Double Page Spread (Untrimmed Bleed)	292 x 456mm
Double Page Spread (Trimmed Bleed)	286 x 450mm

COLOUR SPECIFICATION
Refer to Express Newspapers' Colour Specification Guidelines or contact
Karen Miller.
Inserts
Refer to Express Newspapers' Inserts Guidelines or contact Karen Miller.

Express Newspapers plc
Ludgate House
245 Blackfriars Road
London SE1 9UX
Tel: 0171-928 8000
Fax: 0171-620 1646

Ratecard effective from June 1995

The **F**RANCHISE

FRANCHISE

M A G A Z I N E

`95/`96
Media
Information

Totally targeted readership
all with time, money and
ability to invest

Available at newsagents
nationwide and every
Jobcentre

Over 250,000 prospects
read every edition!

Over 5500 Franchises
already awarded by
advertisers

New Advertising and
Editorial package deals

Many Franchisors rely
entirely on us to achieve
their recruitment goals

Franchise Development Services are the proprietors of. . .

The Franchise Magazine

The very best publication for franchisee recruitment. The vast majority of our 250, 000 readers are keen to own and operate a franchise.

The Franchise Magazine is on sale at newsagents and distributed to Jobcentres throughout the U.K. Bulk subscribers include The Armed Forces, Resettlement Centres, Accountants, Bankers and Professional Advisors.

Many Franchisors receive unprecedented results and trust us with their full franchisee recruitment programme.

The United Kingdom Franchise Directory

Our award winning annual publication is purchased by the most serious prospective franchisees. An enhanced entry will indicate that you are actively recruiting franchisees. Distributed nationwide to all Jobcentres, libraries and on sale at bookshops, it is the fastest selling publication at all franchise exhibitions. Your promotion will ensure a continual flow of enquiries from prospective franchisees who are seeking your particular opportunity.

We also publish:
Franchise International - Quarterly
How to Become a Franchisee - Annually
How to Become a Franchisor - Annually
Asia Franchise Magazine - Quarterly
                    (in Chinese Mandarin)
& Franchise Confidential - Quarterly

1995/6 Advertising Rates

THE FRANCHISE MAGAZINE IS
PUBLISHED QUARTERLY ON
21st MARCH, 21st JUNE, 21st SEPTEMBER
AND 15th DECEMBER BY:

FRANCHISE DEVELOPMENT SERVICES LTD.
CASTLE HOUSE, CASTLE MEADOW,
NORWICH, NR2 1PJ
TEL: 01603 620301 FAX: 01603 630174

All prices are per insertion. They exclude VAT which is
chargeable at the standard rate.

FULL COLOUR

	4 Issues	2/3 Issues	1 Issue
Double Page Spread	£2550	£2750	£2975
Full page	£1425	£1575	£1750
Half Page	£825	£895	£995
Commissioned Editorial			
First page			£1750
Additional Pages			£1250
Full listing (100 words)			£2995

BLACK AND ONE COLOUR

	4 Issues	2/3 Issues	1 Issue
Full Page	£1295	£1395	£1495
Half Page	£795	£875	£975
Quarter Page	£495	£595	£695

MONO

	4 Issues	2/3 Issues	1 Issue
Full Page	£1195	£1295	£1395
Half Page	£695	£795	£895
Quarter Page	£485	£575	£675

FRONT COVER PACKAGE DEAL

Consisting of six pages in total: Front cover in Full
Colour plus four page editorial feature with colour
photographs and a full page colour advertisement.

Package Deal Price: £7500
(Note: Normally booked for 12 months ahead)
Single bookings only and no repeat for 2 years.

Special Positions

	4 Issues	2/3 Issues	1 Issue
First Double Page Spread	£2750	£2975	£3250
Back Cover	£1995	£2150	£2250
Inside Front Cover	£1795	£1895	£1995
Inside Back Cover	£1675	£1765	£1895

All other guaranteed positions - 10% extra
Agency Commission - 10 %
All advertisers payment with order prior to copy
deadline date following booking confirmation and
acceptance by publisher. All advertisement bookings
that are not paid by copy deadline will automatically be
withdrawn.

DIMENSIONS

Double Page Spread	297 x 426mm
Full page	280 x 190mm
Half Page Horizontal	135 x 190mm
Half Page Vertical	280 x 95mm
Quarter Page Vertical	135 x 95mm
Bleed Page	303 x 213mm
Trim Size	297 x 210mm

INSERTS

Low Run Specials	£125.00 per 1000
Full Run	£95.00 per 1000
Minimum 10,000	£950

COPY DEADLINE DATES

Spring 21st February	Autumn 21st August
Summer 21st May	Winter 15th November

FOR FURTHER INFORMATION PLEASE CONTACT YOUR ACCOUNT EXECUTIVE ON:

TEL: 01603 620301

FAX: 01603 630174

Additional Franchise Services. . .

Special Packages by Invitation Only

Talk to us about your total franchise recruitment requirements and we will design a special advertising and editorial package to suit your recruitment goals. These have proved of immense value to many franchisors in the past and continue to prove extremely popular. Obtain further details on request.

Franchise Opportunity Index

Results are virtually guaranteed with this service that provides a continual flow of well qualified prospects. Your franchise description of up to 100 words can be updated as required. This low cost service is £275 per month or £2995 per annum.

Postal Area Marketing (PAM)

Do you have specific geographical areas for development? Is your network more than 50% complete thus making national advertising no longer cost effective? If so, then our PAM service is well worth investigating. From our databank of over 10,000 prospective franchisees we can provide prospects for all 120 postal code regions throughout the United Kingdom. To control your recruitment, call us for further information.

TELEPHONE: 01603 620301 TODAY

CLASSIFIED RATES

Single column cm = £12   Minimum 3 cm = £36

All rates subject to VAT 15%   Series discounts on application

Lineage - 32p per word, minimum £10.   Extras - **BOLD** 80p per word

Cancellations: six weeks prior to booking deadline

EXAMPLE SIZES

4.5 cm

4 cm

Single Column cost £48.00

6 cm

4 cm

Single Column cost £72.00

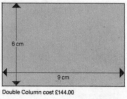

6 cm

9 cm

Double Column cost £144.00

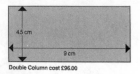

4.5 cm

9 cm

Double Column cost £96.00

CONDITIONS

REMITTANCES: Cheques should be crossed and made payable to AGB Specialist Publications Ltd and sent to Car Mechanics Classified, AGB Specialist Publications Ltd, Audit House, Field End Road, Eastcote, Ruislip, Middlesex HA4 9LT.

IMPORTANT: Whilst every effort is made to ensure that advertisements appear correctly, the Publishers will not be responsible for the consequences arising from errors or delay in publication. It is the advertisers responsibility to check that the first insertion of every series is published correctly and corrections must be notified in time for the second insertion, otherwise the Publishers will not accept liability or offer any reduction in charges.

THE LAW: Advertisers must comply with the Trade Descriptions Act (particularly the description of goods offered for sale) and The Business Advertisements (Disclosures) Order 1977 which requires all advertisements which seek to sell goods in the course of a business to make that fact clear. Readers should be able to tell whether an advertisement relates to a sale by a trader or private seller. It is the responsibility of the advertiser to comply with the order.

MECHANICAL DATA

Whole Page		273×190mm
Half Page		273×92mm or 130×190mm
Quarter Page		130×92mm or 63×190mm
Eighth Page		63mm×92mm
Column Length	266m	Column Width 44mm
Untrimmed WP		306×216mm
DPS type area		273×400mm
WP Bleed		306×216mm
½ page bleed		210×148mm
DPS Bleed		306×432mm
DPS trimmed size		300×213mm
Screen, mono — 100 (40/48 metric) 4 col — 133 (54 metric)		
Positives right reading, emulsion side down		
Web fed, saddle stitched		

CAR MECHANICS

DISPLAY RATES

MONO	1	6	12
Full Page	995	945	896
Full Page FM	1095	1040	985
Half Page	533	506	480
Half Page FM	586	557	528
Quarter Page	278	264	250
Eighth Page	139	132	125

TWO COLOUR			
Full Page	1478	1404	1330
Full Page FM	1626	1545	1463
Half Page	761	723	685
Half Page FM	837	795	753

FOUR COLOUR			
Full Page	1995	1895	1796
Full Page FM	2195	2085	1975
DPS	3990	3791	3591
First DPS Amongst Matter	4190	3980	3771
Half Page	1111	1055	1000
Half Page FM	1222	1161	1100

SPECIAL POSITIONS			
Facing Contents	2294	2180	2065
Outside Back Cover	2294	2180	2065
1st RH Colour	2294	2180	2065
Page 2/3 DPS	4389	4170	3950

INSERT DATA

Loose Cost per thousand subject to checking sample.
Minimum quantity: 40,000.
Print run, maximum 70,000 depending on issue.
Area dictation runs available at extra cost. Ring for quotation.
Bound-in Quotation on request.
Minimum weight of paper for single loose-leaf insert — 135gsm.
A sample of the proposed insert is necessary to check with printers.
Size — not larger than magazine: 295x210mm.
Preferred size no larger than 270x185mm.
Insert can be folded, but if more than one fold, we must have a sample for checking.
Bound-in inserts must be folded. If fold is off-centre, the shorter 'leaf' must be at least 75mm wide (i.e. minimum guard 75mm).
Inserts must be delivered to:

Binder Manager, Chase Web Offset,
Eastern Wood Road, Language Industrial Estate, Plympton,
Plymouth PL7 5ET, Devon. Tel: 0752 345411

Delivery must be at least 20 days before the publication date (our production department will advise). Parcels need to be clearly marked with the client's name, magazine to be inserted in and issue date.

Appendix C: The British Code of Advertising Practice

Principles

2.1 All advertisements should be legal, decent, honest and truthful.

2.2 All advertisements should be prepared with a sense of responsibility to consumers and to society.

2.3 All advertisements should respect the principles of fair competition generally accepted in business.

2.4 No advertisement should bring advertising into disrepute.

2.5 Advertisements must conform with the Codes. Primary responsibility for observing the Codes falls on advertisers. Others involved in preparing and publishing advertisements such as agencies, publishers and other service suppliers also accept an obligation to abide by the Codes.

2.6 Any unreasonable delay in responding to the ASA's enquiries may be considered a breach of the Codes.

2.7 The ASA will on request treat in confidence any private or secret material supplied unless the Courts or officials acting within their statutory powers compel its disclosure.

2.8 The Codes are applied in the spirit as well as in the letter.

Substantiation

3.1 Before submitting an advertisement for publication, advertisers must hold documentary evidence to prove all claims, whether direct or implied, that are capable of objective substantiation. Relevant evidence should be sent without delay if requested by the ASA. The adequacy of evidence will be judged on whether it supports both the detailed claims and the overall impression created by the advertisement.

3.2 If there is a significant division of informed opinion about any claims made in an advertisement they should not be portrayed as universally agreed.

3.3 If the contents of non-fiction books, tapes, videos and the like have not been independently substantiated, advertisements should not exaggerate the value or practical usefulness of their contents.

3.4 Obvious untruths or exaggerations that are unlikely to mislead and incidental minor errors and unorthodox spellings are all allowed provided they do not affect the accuracy or perception of the advertisement in any material way.

Legality

4.1 Advertisers have primary responsibility for ensuring that their advertisements are legal. Advertisements should contain nothing that breaks the law or incites anyone to break it, and should omit nothing that the law requires.

Decency

5.1 Advertisements should contain nothing that is likely to cause serious or widespread offence. Particular care should be taken to avoid causing offence on the grounds of race, religion, sex, sexual orientation or disability. Compliance with the Codes will be judged on the context, medium, audience, product and prevailing standards of decency.

5.2 Advertisements may be distasteful without necessarily conflicting with 5.1 above. Advertisers are urged to consider public sensitivities before using potentially offensive material.

5.3 The fact that a particular product is offensive to some people is not sufficient grounds for objecting to an advertisement for it.

Honesty

6.1 Advertisers should not exploit the credulity, lack of knowledge or inexperience of consumers.

Truthfulness

7.1 No advertisement should mislead by inaccuracy, ambiguity, exaggeration, omission or otherwise.

Matters of opinion

8.1 Advertisers may give a view about any matter, including the qualities or desirability of their products, provided it is clear that they are expressing their own opinion rather than stating a fact. Assertions or comparisons that go beyond subjective opinions are subject to 3.1 above.

Fear and distress

9.1 No advertisement should cause fear or distress without good reason. Advertisers should not use shocking claims or images merely to attract attention.

9.2 Advertisers may use an appeal to fear to encourage prudent behaviour or to discourage dangerous or ill-advised actions; the fear likely to be aroused should not be disproportionate to the risk.

Safety

10.1 Advertisements should not show or encourage unsafe practices except in the context of promoting safety. Particular care should be taken with advertisements addressed to or depicting children and young people.

10.2 Consumers should not be encouraged to drink and drive. Advertisements, including those for breath testing devices, should not suggest that the effects of drinking alcohol can be

masked and should include a prominent warning on the dangers of drinking and driving.

Violence and antisocial behaviour

11.1 Advertisements should contain nothing that condones or is likely to provoke violence or anti-social behaviour.

Political advertising

12.1 Any advertisement whose principal function is to influence opinion in favour of or against any political party or electoral candidate contesting a UK, European parliamentary or local government election, or any matter before the electorate for a referendum, is exempt from clauses 3.1, 7.1, 14.3, 19.2 and 20.1. All other rules in the Codes apply.

12.2 The identity and status of such advertisers should be clear. If their address or other contact details are not generally available they should be included in the advertisement.

12.3 There is a formal distinction between government policy and that of political parties. Advertisements by central or local government, or those concerning government policy as distinct from party policy, are subject to all the Codes rules.

Protection of privacy

13.1 Advertisers are urged to obtain written permission in advance if they portray or refer to individuals or their identifiable possessions in any advertisement. Exceptions include most crowd scenes, portraying anyone who is the subject of the book or film being advertised and depicting property in general outdoor locations.

13.2 Advertisers who have not obtained prior permission from entertainers, politicians, sportsmen and others whose work gives them a high public profile should ensure that they are not portrayed in an offensive or adverse way. Advertisements should not claim or imply an endorsement where none exists.

13.3 Prior permission may not be needed when the advertisement contains nothing that is inconsistent with the position or views of the person featured. Advertisers should be aware that individuals who do not wish to be associated with the advertised product may have a legal claim.

13.4 References to anyone who is deceased should be handled with particular care to avoid causing offence or distress.

13.5 References to members of the Royal Family and the use of the Royal Arms and Emblems are not normally permitted; advertisers should consult the Lord Chamberlain's Office. References to Royal Warrants should be checked with the Royal Warrant Holders' Association.

Testimonials and endorsements

14.1 Advertisers should hold signed and dated proof, including a contact address, for any testimonial they use. Testimonials should be used only with the written permission of those giving them.

14.2 Testimonials should relate to the product being advertised.

14.3 Testimonials alone do not constitute substantiation and the opinions expressed in them must be supported, where necessary, with independent evidence of their accuracy. Any claims based on a testimonial must conform with the Codes.

14.4 Fictitious endorsements should not be presented as though they were genuine testimonials.

14.5 References to tests, trials, professional endorsements, research facilities and professional journals should be used only with the permission of those concerned. They should originate from within the European Union unless otherwise stated in the advertisement. Any establishment referred to should be under the direct supervision of an appropriately qualified professional.

Prices

15.1 Any stated price should be clear and should relate to the product advertised. Advertisers should ensure that prices match the products illustrated.

15.2 Unless addressed exclusively to the trade, prices quoted should include any VAT payable. It should be apparent immediately whether any prices quoted exclude other taxes, duties or compulsory charges and these should, wherever possible, be given in the advertisement.

15.3 If the price of one product is dependent on the purchase of another, the extent of any commitment by consumers should be made clear.

15.4 Price claims such as 'up to' and 'from' should not exaggerate the availability of benefits likely to be obtained by consumers.

Free offers

16.1 There is no objection to making a free offer conditional on the purchase of other items. Consumers' liability for any costs should be made clear in all material featuring the offer. An offer should only be described as free if consumers pay no more than:
a) the current public rates of postage
b) the actual cost of freight or delivery
c) the cost, including incidental expenses, of any travel involved if consumers collect the offer.
Advertisers should make no additional charges for packing and handling.

16.2 Advertisers must not attempt to recover their costs by reducing the quality or composition or by inflating the price of any product that must be purchased as a pre-condition of obtaining another product free.

Availability of products

17.1 Advertisers must make it clear if stocks are limited. Products must not be advertised unless advertisers can demonstrate that they have reasonable grounds for believing that they can satisfy demand. If a product becomes unavailable, advertisers will be required to show evidence of stock monitoring, communications with outlets and the swift withdrawal of advertisements whenever possible.

17.2 Products which cannot be supplied should not normally be advertised as a way of assessing potential demand.

17.3 Advertisers must not use the technique of switch selling, where their sales staff criticise the advertised product or suggest that it is not available and recommend the purchase of a more expensive alternative. They should not place obstacles in the way of purchasing the product or delivering it promptly.

Guarantees

18.1 The full terms of any guarantee should be available for consumers to inspect before they are committed to purchase. Any substantial limitations should be spelled out in the advertisement.

18.2 Advertisers should inform consumers about the nature and extent of any additional rights provided by the guarantee, over and above those given to them by law, and should make clear how to obtain redress.

18.3 'Guarantee' when used simply as a figure of speech should not cause confusion about consumers' legal rights.

Comparisons

19.1 Comparisons can be explicit or implied and can relate to advertisers' own products or to those of their competitors; they are permitted in the interests of vigorous competition and public information.

19.2 Comparisons should be clear and fair. The elements of any comparison should not be selected in a way that gives the advertisers an artificial advantage.

Denigration

20.1 Advertisers should not unfairly attack or discredit other businesses or their products.

20.2 The only acceptable use of another business's broken or defaced products in advertisements is in the illustration of comparative tests, and the source, nature and results of these should be clear.

Exploitation of goodwill

21.1 Advertisers should not make unfair use of the goodwill attached to the trade mark, name, brand, or the advertising campaign of any other business.

Imitation

22.1 No advertisement should so closely resemble any other that it misleads or causes confusion.

Identifying advertisers and recognising advertisements

23.1 Advertisers, publishers and owners of other media should ensure that advertisements are designed and presented in such a way that they can be easily distinguished from editorial.

23.2 Features, announcements or promotions that are disseminated in exchange for a payment or other reciprocal arrangement should comply with the Codes if their content is controlled by the advertisers. They should also be clearly identified and distinguished from editorial (see clause 41).

23.3 Mail order and direct response advertisements and those for one day sales, homework schemes, business opportunities and the like should contain the name and address of the advertisers. Advertisements with a political content should clearly identify their source. Unless required by law, other advertisers are not obliged to identify themselves.

ALCOHOLIC DRINKS

46.1 For the purposes of the Codes, alcoholic drinks are those that exceed 1.2% alcohol by volume.

46.2 The drinks industry and the advertising business accept a responsibility for ensuring that advertisements contain nothing that is likely to lead people to adopt styles of drinking that are unwise. The consumption of alcohol may be portrayed as sociable and thirst-quenching. Advertisements may be humorous, but must still conform with the intention of the rules.

46.3 Advertisements should be socially responsible and should not encourage excessive drinking. Advertisements should not suggest that regular solitary drinking is advisable. Care should be taken not to exploit the young, the immature or those who are mentally or socially vulnerable.

46.4 Advertisements should not be directed at people under eighteen through the selection of media, style of presentation, content or context in which they appear. No medium should be used to advertise alcoholic drinks if more than 25% of its audience is under eighteen years of age.

46.5 People shown drinking should not be, nor should they look, under twenty five. Younger models may be shown in advertisements, for example in the context of family celebrations, but it should be obvious that they are not drinking.

46.6 Advertisements should not feature real or fictitious characters who are likely to appeal particularly to people under eighteen in a way that would encourage them to drink.

46.7 Advertisements should not suggest that any alcoholic drink can enhance mental, physical or sexual capabilities, popularity, attractiveness, masculinity, femininity or sporting achievements.

46.8 Advertisements may give factual information about the alcoholic strength of a drink or its relatively high alcohol content but this should not be the dominant theme of any advertisement. Alcoholic drinks should not be presented as preferable because of their high alcohol content or intoxicating effect.

46.9 Advertisements should not portray drinking alcohol as the main reason for the success of any personal relationship or social event. A brand preference may be promoted as a mark of the drinker's good taste and discernment.

46.10 Drinking alcohol should not be portrayed as a challenge, nor should it be suggested that people who drink are brave, tough or daring for doing so.

46.11 Particular care should be taken to ensure that advertisements for sales promotions requiring multiple purchases do not actively encourage excessive consumption.

48.12 Advertisements should not depict activities or locations where drinking alcohol would be unsafe or unwise. In particular, advertisements should not associate the consumption of alcohol with operating machinery, driving, any activity relating to water or heights, or any other occupation that requires concentration in order to be done safely.

46.13 Low alcohol drinks are those that contain 1.2% alcohol by volume or less. Advertisers should ensure that low alcohol drinks are not promoted in a way that encourages their inappropriate consumption and should not depict activities that require complete sobriety.

CHILDREN

47.1 The way in which children perceive and react to advertisements is influenced by their age, experience and the context in which the message is delivered. The ASA will take these factors into account when assessing advertisements.

47.2 Advertisements and promotions addressed to or featuring children should contain nothing that is likely to result in their physical, mental or moral harm:
a) they should not be encouraged to enter strange places or talk to strangers. Care is needed when they are asked to make collections, enter schemes or gather labels, wrappers, coupons and the like
b) they should not be shown in hazardous situations or behaving dangerously in the home or outside except to promote safety. Children should not be shown unattended in street scenes unless they are old enough to take responsibility for their own safety. Pedestrians and cyclists should be seen to observe the Highway Code
c) they should not be shown using or in close proximity to dangerous substances or equipment without direct adult supervision. Examples include matches, petrol, certain medicines and household substances as well as certain electrical appliances and machinery, including agricultural equipment
d) they should not be encouraged to copy any practice that might be unsafe for a child.

47.3 Advertisements and promotions addressed to or featuring children should not exploit their credulity, loyalty, vulnerability or lack of experience:
a) they should not be made to feel inferior or unpopular for not buying the advertised product
b) they should not be made to feel that they are lacking in courage, duty or loyalty if they do not buy or do not encourage others to buy a particular product
c) it should be made easy for them to judge the size, characteristics and

performance of any product advertised and to distinguish between real-life situations and fantasy

d) parental permission should be obtained before they are committed to purchasing complex and costly goods and services.

47.4 Advertisements and promotions addressed to children:

a) should not actively encourage them to make a nuisance of themselves to parents or others

b) should not make a direct appeal to purchase unless the product is one that would be likely to interest children and that they could reasonably afford. Mail order advertisers should take care when using youth media not to promote products that are unsuitable for children

c) should not exaggerate what is attainable by an ordinary child using the product being advertised or promoted

d) should not actively encourage them to eat or drink at or near bedtime, to eat frequently throughout the day or to replace main meals with confectionery or snack foods

e) should not exploit their susceptibility to charitable appeals and should explain the extent to which their participation will help in any charity-linked promotions.

47.5 Promotions addressed to children:

a) should not encourage excessive purchases in order to participate

b) should make clear that parental permission is required if prizes and incentives might cause conflict between children and their parents. Examples include animals, bicycles, tickets for outings, concerts and holidays

c) should clearly explain the number and type of any additional proofs of purchase needed to participate

d) should contain a prominent closing date

e) should not exaggerate the value of prizes or the chances of winning them.

MOTORING

48.1 Advertisements for motor vehicles, fuel or accessories should avoid portraying or referring to practices that encourage antisocial behaviour.

48.2 Advertisers should not make speed or acceleration claims the predominant message of their advertisements. However it is legitimate to give general information about a vehicle's performance such as acceleration statistics, braking power, roadholding and top and mid-range speeds.

48.3 Advertisers should not portray speed in a way that might encourage motorists to drive irresponsibly or to break the law.

48.4 Vehicles should not be depicted in dangerous or unwise situations in a way that would encourage irresponsible driving. Their capabilities may be demonstrated on a track or circuit provided it is clearly not in use as a public highway.

48.5 Care should be taken in cinema advertisements and those in electronic media where the moving image may give the impression of exceptional speed. In all cases where vehicles are shown in normal driving circumstances on the public road they should be seen not to exceed UK speed limits.

48.6 When making environmental claims for their products, advertisers should conform with the Specific Rules on Environmental Claims.

48.7 Prices quoted should correspond to the vehicles illustrated. For example, it is not acceptable to feature only a top-of-the-range model alongside the starting price for that range.

48.8 Safety claims should not exaggerate the benefit to consumers. Advertisers should not make absolute claims about safety unless they hold evidence to support them.

ENVIRONMENTAL CLAIMS

49.1 The basis of any claim should be explained clearly and should be qualified where necessary. Unqualified claims can mislead if they omit significant information.

49.2 Claims such as 'environmentally friendly' or 'wholly biodegradable' should not be used without qualification unless advertisers can provide convincing evidence that their product will cause no environmental damage. Qualified claims and comparisons such as 'greener' or 'friendlier' may be acceptable if advertisers can substantiate that their product provides an overall improvement in environmental terms either against their competitors' or their own previous products.

49.3 Where there is a significant division of scientific opinion or where evidence is inconclusive this should be reflected in any statements made in the advertisement. Advertisers should not suggest that their claims command universal acceptance if it is not the case.

49.4 If a product has never had a demonstrably adverse effect on the environment, advertisements should not imply that the formulation has changed to make it safe. It is legitimate, however, to make claims about a product whose composition has changed or has always been designed in a way that omits chemicals known to cause damage to the environment.

49.5 The use of extravagant language should be avoided, as should bogus and confusing scientific terms. If it is necessary to use a scientific expression, its meaning should be clear.

HEALTH & BEAUTY PRODUCTS AND THERAPIES
General

50.1 Medical and scientific claims made about beauty and health-related products should be backed by trials, where appropriate conducted on people. Substantiation will be assessed by the ASA on the basis of established scientific knowledge.

50.2 Advertisers should not discourage people from having essential treatment; medical advice is needed for serious or prolonged ailments and advertisers should not offer medicines or therapies for them.

50.3 Advice, diagnosis or treatment of any serious medical condition should be conducted face-to-face. Advertisers inviting consumers to diagnose their own minor ailments should not make claims that might lead to a mistaken diagnosis.

50.4 Consumers should not be encouraged to use products to excess and advertisers should not suggest that their products or therapies are guaranteed to work, absolutely safe or without side-effects for everyone.

50.5 Advertisements should not suggest that any product is safe or effective merely because it is 'natural' or that it is generally safer because it omits an ingredient in common use.

50.6 Advertisers offering individual treatments, particularly those that are physically invasive, may be asked by the media and the ASA to provide full details together with information about those who will supervise and administer them. Where appropriate, practitioners should have relevant and recognised qualifications. Consumers should be encouraged to take independent medical advice before committing themselves to significant treatments.

50.7 References to the relief of symptoms or the superficial signs of ageing are acceptable if they can be substantiated. Unqualified claims such as 'cure' and 'rejuvenation' are not generally acceptable.

50.8 Claims made for the treatment of minor addictions and bad habits should make clear the vital role of willpower.

50.9 Advertisers should not use unfamiliar scientific words for common conditions.

Medicines

50.10 The Medicines Act 1968 and its regulations, as well as regulations implementing European Community Directive 92/28/EEC, govern the advertising and promotion of medicines and the conditions of ill health that they can be offered to treat. Guidance on the legislation is available from the Medicines Control Agency (MCA).

50.11 Medicines must be licensed by the MCA before they are advertised and any claims made for products must conform with the licence. Unlicensed products should not make medicinal claims. Advertisements should refer to the MCA, the licence or the EC only if required to do so by the MCA.

50.12 Prescription-only medicines may not be advertised to the public. Health-related claims in advertisements and promotions addressed only to the medical and allied professions are exempt from the Codes.

50.13 Advertisements should include the name of the product, an indication of what it is for, text such as 'Always read the label' and the common name of the active ingredient if there is only one. There should be no suggestion that any medicine is either a food or a cosmetic.

50.14 Advertisers must not use fear or anxiety to promote medicines or recovery from illness and should not suggest that using or avoiding a product can affect normal good health.

50.15 Illustrations of the effect or action of any product on the human body should be accurate.

50.16 Advertisements for medicines should not be addressed to children.

50.17 Advertisers should not use health professionals or celebrities to endorse medicines.

50.18 Advertisements for any medicine should not claim that its effects are as good as or better than those of another identifiable product.

50.19 Homeopathic medicinal products must be registered in the UK. Any product information given in the advertisement should be confined to what appears on the label. Advertisements should include a warning to consult a doctor if-symptoms persist and should not make any medicinal or therapeutic claims or refer to any ailment.

Vitamins, minerals and food supplements

50.20 Advertisers should hold scientific evidence for any claim that their vitamin or mineral product or food supplement is beneficial to health.

50.21 A well-balanced diet should provide the vitamins and minerals needed each day by a normal, healthy individual. Advertisers may offer supplements as a safeguard, but should not suggest that there is widespread vitamin or mineral deficiency or that it is necessary or therapeutic to augment a well-balanced diet. Advertisements should not imply that supplements will guard against deficiency, elevate mood or enhance performance. Supplements should not be promoted as a substitute for a healthy diet.

50.22 Certain groups of people may benefit from vitamin and mineral supplementation. These include people who eat nutritionally inadequate meals, the elderly, children and adolescents, convalescents, athletes in training, those who are physically very active, women of child-bearing age, lactating and pregnant women and dieters. In assessing claims the ASA will bear in mind recommendations made by the Department of Health.

50.23 Serious vitamin and mineral depletion caused by illness should be diagnosed and treated by a doctor. Self-medication should not be promoted on the basis that it will influence the speed or extent of recovery.

Cosmetics

50.24 Claims made about the action that a cosmetic has on or in the skin should distinguish between the composition of the product and any effects brought about by the way in which it is applied, such as massage. Scientific evidence should also make this distinction.

50.25 Some cosmetics have an effect on the kind of skin changes that are caused by environmental factors. Advertisements for them can therefore refer to temporarily preventing, delaying or masking premature ageing.

Hair and scalp

50.26 Advertisers should be able to provide scientific evidence, where appropriate in the form of trials conducted on people, for any claim that their product or therapy can prevent baldness or slow it down, arrest or reverse hair loss, stimulate or improve hair growth, nourish hair roots, strengthen the hair or improve its health as distinct from its appearance.

EMPLOYMENT AND BUSINESS OPPORTUNITIES

54.1 Advertisers should distinguish clearly between offers of employment and business opportunities. Before publication, media normally require full details of the advertisers and any terms and conditions imposed on respondents.

54.2 Employment advertisements must correspond to genuine vacancies and potential employees must not be asked to send money for further details. Living and working conditions should not be misrepresented. Quoted earnings should be precise; if a forecast has to be made this should not be unrepresentative. If income is earned from a basic salary and commission, commission only, or in some other way, this should be made clear.

54.3 An employment agency must make clear in advertisements that it is an employment agency.

54.4 Homework schemes require participants to make articles, perform services or offer facilities at or from home. Consumers should be given:

a) the full name and address of the advertisers

b) a clear description of the work; the support available to homeworkers should not be exaggerated

c) an indication of whether participants are self-employed or employed by a business

d) the likely level of earnings, but only if this can be supported with evidence of the experience of current homeworkers

e) no forecast of earnings if the scheme is new

f) details of any required investment or binding obligation

g) details of any charges for raw materials, machines, components, administration and the like

h) information on whether the advertisers will buy back any goods made

i) any limitations or conditions that might influence consumers prior to their decision to participate.

54.5 Advertisements for business opportunities should contain:

a) the name and contact details of the advertisers

b) where possible, a clear description of the work involved and the extent of investors' commitments, including any financial investment; the support available should not be exaggerated

c) no unrepresentative or exaggerated earnings figures.

54.6 Vocational training and other instruction courses should make no promises of employment unless it is guaranteed. The duration of the course and the level of attainment needed to embark on it should be made clear.

54.7 The sale of directories giving details of employment or business opportunities should indicate plainly the nature of what is being offered.

FINANCIAL SERVICES AND PRODUCTS

55.1 The rules that follow provide only general guidance. Advertisers, their agencies and the media must also comply with the numerous statutes that govern financial services and products including issuing advertisements, investment opportunities, credit facilities and the provision of financial information.

55.2 Offers of financial services and products should be set out in a way that allows them to be understood easily by the audience being addressed. Advertisers should ensure that they do not take advantage of people's inexperience or gullibility.

55.3 Advertisers asking for a commitment at a distance should make sure that their full address is given outside any response coupon or other mechanism.

55.4 Advertisements should indicate the nature of the contract being offered, any limitations, expenses, penalties and charges and the terms of withdrawal. Alternatively, where an advertisement is short or general in its content, free explanatory material giving full details of the offer should be readily available before a binding contract is entered into.

55.5 The basis used to calculate any rates of interest, forecasts or projections should be apparent immediately.

55.6 Advertisements should make clear that the value of investments is variable and, unless guaranteed, can go down as well as up. If the value of the investment is guaranteed details should be included in the advertisement.

55.7 Advertisements should specify that past performance or experience does not necessarily give a guide for the future. Any examples used should not be unrepresentative.

(Reproduced by kind permission of the Advertising Standards Authority. Further details about the Act can be obtained from: The Advertising Standards Authority Ltd, 2 Torrington Place, London WC1E 7HW.)

Appendix D:
Useful contacts

Advertising Association, Abford House, 15 Wilton Road, London SW1V 1NJ. Telephone: 0171-828 2771.

Advertising Standards Authority Limited, Brook House, 2-16 Torrington Place, London WC1E 7HN. Telephone: 0171-580 5555.

Association of British Chambers of Commerce, Tufton Street, London SW1P 3QB. Telephone: 0171-222 1555.

Association of Illustrators, 1 Colville Place, London W1P 1HN. Telephone: 0171-636 4100.

Association of Market Survey Organisations Limited, 16 Creighton Avenue, London N10 1NU. Telephone: 0181-444 3692.

Association of Media Independents Limited, 48 Percy Road, London N12 8BU. Telephone: 0181- 343 7779.

Audit Bureau of Circulation Limited, Black Prince Yard, 207 High Street, Berkhamsted, Hertfordshire HP4 1AD. Telephone 01442 870800.

British Business Press, Imperial House, 15-19 Kingsway, London WC2B 6UN. Telephone: 0171-379 6268.

British Institute of Professional Photography, 2 Amwell End, Ware, Hertfordshire SG1 2HN. Telephone: 01920 464011.

British Printing Industries Federation, 11 Bedford Row, London WC1R 4DX. Telephone: 0171-242 6904.

Bulk Verified Services, Black Prince Yard, 207 High Street, Berkhamsted, Hertfordshire HP4 1AD. Telephone: 01442 870800.

CBD Research Limited, 15 Wickham Road, Beckenham, Kent BR3 2JS. Telephone: 0181-650 7745.

Central Statistical Office, Great George Street, London SW1P 3AQ. Telephone: 0171-270 3000.

Committee of Advertising Practice, Brook House, 2-16 Torrington Place, London WC1E 7HN. Telephone: 0171-580 5555.

Directory Publishers Association, 93a Blenheim Crescent, London W11 2EG. Telephone: 0171-221 9089.

Her Majesty's Stationery Office, St Crispins, Duke Street, Norwich, Norfolk NR3 1PD. Telephone: 01603 622211.

Incorporated Society of British Advertisers Limited, 44 Hertford Street, London W1Y 8AE. Telephone: 0171-499 7502.

Institute of Practitioners in Advertising, 44 Belgrave Square, London SW1X 8QS. Telephone: 0171-235 7020.

Joint Industry Committee for National Readership Surveys, 44 Belgrave Square, London SW1X 8QS. Telephone: 0171-235 7020.

London Business School, Sussex Place, Regents Park, London NW1 4SA. Telephone: 0171-262 5050.

Maclean Hunter Limited, 33–39 Bowling Green Lane, London EC1R 0DA. Telephone: 0171-508 8000.

Market Research Society, 15 Northburgh Street, London EC1V 0AH. Telephone: 0171-490 4911.

Media Audits Limited, 16 Dufors Place, London W1V 1FE. Telephone: 0171-734 4080.

Media Expenditure Analysis Limited, Register House, 4 Holford Yard, Cruickshank Street, London WC1X 9HD. Telephone: 0171-833 1212.

Newspaper Publishers Association, 34 Southwark Bridge Road, London SE1 9EU. Telephone: 0171-928 6928.

Newspaper Society, Bloomsbury House, Bloomsbury Square, 74-77 Great Russell Street, London WC1B 3DA. Telephone: 0171-636 7014.

Periodical Publishers Association, Imperial House, 15-19 Kingsway, London WC2B 6UN. Telephone: 0171-379 6268.

Science Reference Library, 25 Southampton Buildings, Chancery Lane, London WC2A 1AN. Telephone: 0171-405 8721.

Society of Typographic Designers, 21-27 Seagrave Road, London SW6 1RP. Telephone: 0171-381 4258.

Verified Free Distribution Limited, Black Prince Yard, 207 High Street, Berkhamsted, Hertfordshire HP4 1AD. Telephone: 01442 870800.

Appendix E:
Recommended reading

There are many publications available which are helpful when planning an advertising campaign within the press. The following are especially relevant:

Books

A Practical Guide to Project Planning by Celia Burton and Norma Michael, £14.95. Published by Kogan Page Limited, 120 Pentonville Road, London N1 9JN. Telephone: 0171-278 0433. This is an extremely useful read for all prospective press advertisers. It will enable you to assess your forthcoming activities in a full and effective manner.

The Effective Use of Market Research by Robin Birn, £12.95. Published by Kogan Page Limited, 120 Pentonville Road, London N1 9JN. Telephone: 0171-278 0433. A good book for anyone who is not yet wholly familiar with the do's and don't's of market research. It tackles the subject in a clear and sensible manner which is easy to absorb and understand.

Researching Business Markets edited by Ken Sutherland, £19.95. Published by Kogan Page Limited, 120 Pentonville Road, London N1 9JN. Telephone: 0171-278 0433. This practical handbook is a first-class introduction to marketing research, describing all of the various techniques and their particular strengths and weaknesses. It should enable you to become a more informed research buyer and user.

Budgeting by Terry Dickey, £9.99. Published by Kogan Page Limited, 120 Pentonville Road, London N1 9JN. Telephone: 0171-278 0433. A readable book which should help you in your financial planning for press advertising activities. A sensible and informative buy.

Creative People by Winston Fletcher, £14.95. Published by Random House, 20 Vauxhall Bridge Road, London SW1V 2SA. Telephone: 0171-973 9670. This guide examines the relationship between creative people and their employers. Although it is not directed at advertisers planning to work alongside illustrators, photographers and copywriters, it may help you to make the most of advertising agency staff, and to understand them better.

The Secrets of Successful Copywriting by Patrick Quinn, £8.95. Published by Butterworth Heinemann Limited, Linacre House, Jordan Hill, Oxford OX2 8DP. Telephone: 01865 311366. Despite the author's offbeat and whimsical writing style, this book is packed full of excellent advice and valuable, worked-through examples, showing you how to create quality advertisements for your press campaign.

Law and the Media by Tom Crone, £14.95. Published by Butterworth Heinemann Limited, Linacre House, Jordan Hill, Oxford OX2 8DP. Telephone: 01865 311366. An everyday guide for professionals which is sufficiently jargon-free and down-to-earth to be a first-rate addition to the would-be advertiser's book collection. It is worth referring to prior to advertising activities.

Magazines
Campaign, £1.85 for one copy, £85 per year. Published by Haymarket Campaign Magazines Limited, 22 Lancaster Gate, London W2 3LY. Telephone: 0171-413 4570. A weekly magazine which is the bible of the advertising industry. Looked at by publishers, advertising agencies and advertisers alike, this ought to be required reading for everyone entering the field.

Creative Review, £3.45 per single copy, £38 for one year. Published by Centaur Communications Limited, St Giles House, 50 Poland Street, London W1V 4AX. Telephone: 0171-439 4222. This is a monthly magazine that is worth checking out – it is full of fascinating articles and good advice which could help to improve your own advertising ideas.

Miscellaneous Publications
British Rate and Data, £130 per copy, £331 for one year. Published by Maclean Hunter Limited, 33 Bowling Green Lane, London EC1R 0DA. Telephone: 0171-505 8000. A 600-page directory published every month, and which includes data about most of the many types of publication that are known collectively as 'the press'. Even if you read nothing else about advertising, take a look at this.

Please note that books should be available from your local bookshop and/or library. Contact the appropriate publishers if difficulties arise. Ask for complimentary copies of magazines from the relevant publishers and subsequently take out annual subscriptions if you think they would be of ongoing use. All prices quoted are believed to be correct for 1 January 1996, but are liable to change in due course.

Glossary

Many of the terms used in this book are self-explanatory – advertising agency, editorial department, subscriptions, and the like. Others are less so and are included here.

À la carte agency. Advertising agency which produces advertisements but which does not usually participate in media planning, negotiating and purchasing. Also known as a 'creative agency'.

ABC Certificate. Audit Bureau of Circulation Ltd Certificate, verifying the average number of copies of a publication sold or distributed.

Accounts executive. Essentially a sales representative acting for an advertising agency or publication.

Advertorial. Article which appears to be written independently of the nearby advertisement, but is in fact related advertising material.

Appropriation. Sum of money set aside for advertising activities. Better known as a budget.

Bleed off. Extension of text and/or illustrations to the edge of the page.

Block. Etched plate used during printing processes.

Bromide. Photographic print on bromide paper.

Budget. See 'Appropriation'.

BVS Certificate. Bulk Verified Services Certificate, verifying the average number of copies of a free publication distributed in bulk. See also VFD Certificate.

Camera ready. Text and illustrations ready for production.

Circulation. The number of copies of an issue of a publication sold, delivered or handed out.

Classified advertisement. Line-by-line advertisement beneath a general heading such as 'Employment Opportunities'. Relatively inexpensive.

Consumer-specific title. Magazine for special interest groups, such as sci-fi enthusiasts.

Controlled circulation. Method of circulation whereby titles are sent to a limited number of named individuals.

Copy. Another name for text. Often used to describe text and illustrations together.

Copy deadline. Date (and time) by which copy must be submitted for publication.

Copywriter. Creative person responsible for producing the text of advertisements.

Cost per thousand. The cost of reaching every 1,000 people within a publication's circulation.

Creative agency. See 'À la carte agency'.

Demographics. Study of the make-up of a population, by age, sex, and so on.

Display advertisement. Bordered advertisement, often large and relatively costly.

Double-page spread. Two, side-by-side pages. More often referred to as 'a DPS'.

Ear. Space to the side of the front page title. Also known as an 'ear piece' or 'ear spec', or referred to as the 'title cover'.

Ear piece. See 'ear'.
Ear spec. See 'ear'.

Face. A type design.
Facing matter. The material facing a particular position in a publication. Sometimes abbreviated to 'FM'.
Full service agency. Advertising agency able to plan and conduct an advertising campaign from beginning to end.

Gatefold. Sheet with folded-in leaves.
General consumer magazine. Publication of interest to most sectors of the population.
Gravure. Method of printing.

Insert. Item inserted into a publication, either loose or bound in.
Island position. Distinctive but often expensive position surrounded by editorial text.

Key. Identifying element specific to a particular advertisement enabling the response to it to be monitored accurately.

Letterpress. Method of printing.
Linage. The cost per line of a classified advertisement. Also known as 'line rate'.
Line rate. See 'Linage'.
Litho. Method of printing.

Marketing guide. Comprehensive information pack about a publication. Well worth studying. Also called a 'Media guide' or 'Media pack'.
Media independent. Advertising agency which deals with the planning and purchase of advertising space and time. It does not offer creative services.
Media guide. See 'Marketing guide'.
Media pack. See 'Marketing guide'.
Mono. Black and white only.

Next matter. The material next to a particular position in a publication. May be abbreviated to 'NM'.

Pass-on readership. The total number of people who look at a copy of a publication.
Penetration. The extent to which a publication reaches an advertiser's target audience.
Profile. The make-up of a publication's readership, by age, sex, social grade and so on.
Proofs. Copies of material produced for checking prior to amendments and production of the final version.

Rate card. Sheet or pamphlet listing advertising and other data about a publication. Usually included in a marketing guide, or on its own.
Run of paper. Situation whereby material will be placed anywhere within a newspaper, at the publisher's discretion. Also referred to as 'Run of press' or 'ROP'.
Run of press. See 'Run of paper'.
Run of week. Situation whereby material will be published at some time during a week, at the publisher's discretion. Also known as 'ROW'.

Semi-display advertisement. Display advertisement located in the classified section of a publication.
Single column centimetre. Unit of sale, one column wide by one centimetre deep. Normally abbreviated to 'SCC'.
Single spot. One colour which may be added to an advertisement, sometimes referred to as 'Spot colour'.
Social grades. Classification of the population based on the occupation of the head of the household.
Solus position. Situation whereby an advertisement is the only one on a page.
Special position. Guaranteed position for an advertisement, as chosen by the advertiser.
Spot colour. See 'Single spot'.

Type area. Part of page covered by text and illustrations.

Typesetter. Person responsible for setting text and illustrations onto printed pages.

Title cover. See 'Ear'.

Voucher copy. Complimentary copy of a publication given to an individual or organization advertising within it.

VFD Certificate. Verified Free Distribution Certificate confirming the average number of copies of a publication distributed freely.

Index